*STUDIES IN SCRIPTURE
AND ITS AUTHORITY*

STUDIES IN SCRIPTURE AND ITS AUTHORITY

by

Herman Ridderbos

William B. Eerdmans Publishing Company

The essays in this book are revised versions of lectures
originally given in Grand Rapids, Michigan, under the
sponsorship of the Calvin Foundation.

Library of Congress Cataloging in Publication Data

Ridderbos, Herman N.
  Studies in Scripture and its authority.

  Revised versions of lectures given under the sponsorship of the Calvin
Foundation.
  1. Bible — Inspiration — Addresses, essays, lectures. 2. Bible — Evi-
dences, authority, etc. — Addresses, essays, lectures. 3. Bible. N.T. Gospels
— Criticism, interpretation, etc. — Addresses, essays, lectures. I. Title.
BS480.R517   220.1'3   77-13206
ISBN 0-8028-1707-6

Contents

A Note to the Reader

SERIOUS STUDENTS of the Bible and concerned church members will welcome the appearance in print of these helpful and interesting essays by Professor Ridderbos. In a day when the interpretation of Scripture is often undertaken apart from a commitment to the church, the author of this book is well known to have matched a place of eminence in the world of biblical scholarship with widespread esteem as a dedicated churchman. It is his experience in the latter context that forms the arena for his discussion in these six chapters.

Professor Ridderbos is keenly aware of the issues of belief which trouble the church today. It is his conviction that honestly facing these questions can strengthen the faith of the church and make it more responsive to the needs of the world in which it is called to speak the clear word of Good News. Here, then, are candid and lucid discussions of such disputed topics as the doctrine of Scripture, the person of Christ, the kingdom of God, and the last things. In all of these areas the tension between the "human" element and the "divine" has historically been a source of disagreement. The stress in recent thought has been laid on the human side, with often disconcerting and sometimes devastating results for the peace of the church. Yet the concerns behind these issues may not be ignored out of a false hope that everything will thus be settled.

We are grateful for the opportunity presented by the Calvin Foundation to offer these contributions by Professor Ridderbos to a wider reading public.

THE PUBLISHERS.

1.

New Developments in
Church and Theology

IT IS A COMMONPLACE that the church and theology of
today are involved in extensive and deep-seated change, a process which may indeed be described as a crisis. This development is reflected in a kind of thinking and living frequently
characterized as secular or worldly. The idea of another world
than that in which we live and work and die is losing its
reality. The way God is involved in what happens in this
world is more and more becoming a problem for many people.

This phenomenon, of course, is not new. Since the dawn
of what is called the modern age, the process of secularization
in living and thinking has made a tremendous impact on
what had until then been considered as the Christian world
and Christian civilization. But recently a lot of factors have
worked together to accelerate the process in an unprecedented
way. Those factors are not only theoretical and spiritual.
Secularization is a result of our very way of life in today's
society. Modern techniques automate human life, accelerate
our tempo of living and working, subject us to fixed sched-
ules and programs, allow less and less room for individuality
and personal initiative, further spiritual superficiality, and
form a constant threat to personal spiritual life.

The immediate, direct knowledge of what happens in the
world by way of mass communication has a kaleidoscope
effect: all kinds of images tumble through one another. We
cannot discern the contexts; we stare at unimaginable problems which we cannot solve; we see the discrepancies in human life in their worldwide proportions; we are confronted

with the sufferings of millions of people. We switch off the television and radio, because we cannot digest it emotionally. How can we bring all this into relation with God? How can we absorb all this in the closed circuit of an all-embracing perspective of faith? I cannot offer a philosophical analysis of all this, but I do understand that it forms a real threat to our Christian manner of thinking, and, indeed, to our Christian faith itself.

To be sure, reactions differ. Many people, especially older ones, experience these developments with opposition in their hearts. It is as if all the protective walls around them have been demolished, as if they are standing in a frigid blast of wind against which they have to shield themselves without the help of the old, traditional certainties. They feel that they cannot face the new problems adequately and at the same time they do not want to adapt themselves to a form of secular thinking which contradicts not only their tradition but also their deepest Christian conviction.

On the other side many people are convinced that church and theology can only survive if they are willing to reconsider their old positions in a very radical way. It is not only the old terminology, not only the schemes and subjects by which the church used to present and express its confession, which are to be abandoned in order to meet the challenge of the time. Even more has to be done. The question of what the presuppositions and criteria of Christian faith and Christian religion and of religion itself are, is to be answered in a new way. Instead of the scrupulous caution of the conservative way of thinking and living, a new consciousness of freedom and courage has to take possession of church and theology. Only in this radical way will church and theology be able to stay in the center of human life and culture instead of surviving as a mere worthless relic of what has gone by forever.

It is worthwhile to give due attention to this new approach, this "new theology," as it is already being called. What does it mean? How is it to be defined? Are we confronted here with a new form of the old liberalism? Many will contest this and maintain that this is not the case and certainly not the intention. What is intended, rather, is to give real answers to real questions raised by real people in our time. Again and again you hear of the need for that which is "understandable" and "relevant" for our day. Traditional theology — so it is said — does not reach the person of today, even if he is religious. Traditional theology gives answers, even clear answers, but not answers which match the questions that are asked today. And so a new explanation, a new hermeneutic of the message of the Bible, is necessary.

To move beyond generalities, I should like to elucidate and discuss this issue in three important areas: the doctrine of Scripture, the doctrine of Christ, and the doctrine of the kingdom of God.

* * *

With regard to the Bible more and more emphasis is being given to what is called the indirect character of revelation. In the Bible, it is said, we are confronted with the Word of God, but with the Word of God as it was understood and interpreted by certain people at a certain time in human history. Similarly, we encounter divine salvation there. And in a sense this salvation does not change, because Jesus Christ the Savior is the same, yesterday, today, and forever. But we are other than the people of the Bible, and we can understand things only out of our own cultural, social, and anthropological presuppositions, our own spiritual environment and horizon, just as people in the Bible did. Therefore, the argument runs, we are not bound to their interpretations of and reflections on salvation. What the Bible means by "salvation," "reconciliation," "resurrection," "kingdom of God," what is expressed in the biblical titles of Jesus (Messiah, Son of God, Son of Man) might have a different meaning for us from what was meant for people two thousand years ago.

Jesus himself is normative, and the New Testament writings are the sources from which we are to know him. But the *con-*

ception of salvation and the *way* Jesus is presented to us are
not normative. Even in the gospels, the "historical" Jesus is
reflected only very vaguely, and the real Jesus only in the
ideas and conceptions of salvation of the evangelists and the
early church. Therefore the Bible, on this interpretation, is
totally human, a book about what men have experienced and
have interpreted as revelation and as the Word of God in
their lives. We are in a new situation. We have to give our
own interpretations of what we can distinguish indirectly in
their words and witness as the Word of God for us. This is
seen as the consequence of the indirect character of revelation and of the human character of the interpretation of the
Word of God in Scripture.

It is not easy to pass a quick judgment on this evaluation of
the Scriptures. As a matter of fact, Reformed theology has
always spoken of the humanity of Scripture, at least of the
"human factor" in it. Although this terminology is not ir-
reproachable, it did express in a certain way that the divine
word has entered into the words of men, and not only in their
words, but also in their mind and into their time. This mind
cannot be separated from its humanity, nor this time from its
temporality, which is to say, from its transitoriness. *Finitum
non capax infiniti:* the finite cannot comprehend the infinite,
nor the human the divine. Thus the important question is not
whether the Word of God has or has not come to us through
the temporal prism of the human word and the human spirit.
It has. To speak of the indirectness of the divine word is
something like describing the dispersion of light through a
spectrum. The light remains the same, but the spectrum
changes. The society of ancient Israel is a different band of
the spectrum from that of our society. The same holds true of
the Roman culture in which Paul lived. Therefore the old
commandments, for example, about waging wars in the Book
of Deuteronomy, or about the place of slaves and the behavior
of women in the New Testament, are not simply applicable
to our situation. For the old society is gone. The light still
shines, but in another band of the spectrum.

We can go on with further examples. For instance, we encounter psychological and anthropological concepts in the Bible, such as "mind," "soul," "body," some of which cannot even be translated in our languages. We do not have adequate concepts for them, because we have in some respects other conceptions of the inner life, of the relation of "soul," "spirit," and "body," and about the very idea of what "body" is.

Study of the Bible leads us on to the insight that there is variety in the way salvation is explained and interpreted in the Scriptures. This is apparent not only when we compare the letters of Paul with others in the New Testament, which do not display the profound and rich thought of the great apostle, but even when we study the four gospels. Each gospel writer appears to have his own point of view; he arranges, interprets the gospel material in his own way, in an attempt to bring to expression the glory of Jesus as well and as appropriately as possible, with regard to his own specific purpose. This, of course, also depends on human potential, character, situation, horizon.

What has been called the "organic" (*not* "mechanical") character of inspiration appears increasingly to display a lot of facets. Much remains for the attentive reader of the Bible to learn; this pluriformity of interpretation of salvation in Scripture should not, however, distress and disappoint but surprise and astonish him with the manifold grace of God. This might leave the impression that the Bible is in many respects very human and time-bound. But the question remains whether the Bible thus loses its character and authority for us as the book of God's revelation.

To say that revelation in the Bible has come to us in human language and human attire and that it adapts itself to the human situation in which it has to function is totally different from saying that the Bible contains only pious, faithful, but nevertheless human reactions and interpretations of the revelation, which are *as such* subjected to our faith-criticism. In the former case the Bible itself is for us the word of revelation. Even then we are allowed — indeed, committed —

to ask, in the light of the Scripture itself and according to the old adage that Scripture is its own interpreter, what is meant for all times and all peoples, and what is not. But this may not detract from the authority of the Word of God which has been spoken by his prophets and apostles and by Jesus Christ himself. This authority, however it is further defined, represents the absolutely unique character of the Bible as the word and the interpretation of the Word of God.

On the other hand, if the Bible is no more than human reaction to and interpretation of what men understood as God's revelation to them, we may approach this interpretation with respect and appreciation, but need accord it no more authority than that of other interpretations of the revelation, of church fathers, theologians, and pious men and women in the history of church. The Bible then is only unique to the extent that its writers were nearer in time to the source of revelation.

There can be no doubt which of these two positions is that of Scripture itself. The Bible does not qualify itself as a book of testimonies of faith and interpretations of faith, which may as well be respected as criticized. As a matter of fact, such an approach is recommended by Paul with regard to prophetical utterances in the Christian congregation: "Do not quench the Spirit, do not despise prophesying, but test everything; hold fast what is good, abstain from every form of evil" (1 Thess. 5:19ff.) — a beautiful example of a generous and at the same time critical approach. But with regard to the Scripture of the Old Testament and to his own apostolic witness Paul speaks in a totally different way. In the same letter he writes: "And we also thank God constantly for this, that when you received the word of God which you heard from us, you accepted it not as the word of men but as what it really is, the word of God" (1 Thess. 2:13). Similarily, in a text in which the interpretation of Scripture itself is at stake (2 Peter 1:20, 21) there is an explicit warning against arbitrary interpretation of Scripture, interpretation that does not take into account that Scripture is not human but divine in its origin, and that the explanation must therefore be subjected to

Scripture itself: "First of all you must understand this, that no prophecy of scripture is a matter of one's own interpretation, because no prophecy ever came by the impulse of man, but men moved by the Holy Spirit spoke from God."

This is not just a matter of so-called formal or external authority. It has its very right and reason in the fact that Scripture in all its variety, in all its changing approaches and different interpretations, does confront us with God's revelation in Jesus Christ. Therefore Scripture can say that, whatever may change in life, the Word of God is everlasting. To be sure, this is not to be taken in an atomistic or fragmentary sense, nor on the other hand as an ideal truth that everyone in each generation has to explain for himself; but, as Scripture says, as the word which was preached to you (1 Pet. 1:25). And this is the word of and about Jesus Christ, who is the same, yesterday, today, and for eternity.

This does not mean, of course, that every time and generation has to give the same answers when confronted with the Scriptures. As we already saw, the Bible itself includes various interpretations of salvation. Life is changing and people are changing in their different situations; and the reality of God's revelation is more than one prophet or apostle can bring to expression. And if Jesus Christ is the Savior of all generations, in whom are hidden all the treasures of wisdom and knowledge, then the contents of the Christian message will always appear to have new answers to new questions.

But at the same time Jesus Christ is the same, and his salvation is the same. That presupposes too that amidst all human developments man himself basically does not alter with respect to what he needs for salvation. The dominant clue for all interpretation of Scripture is thus Christ, not man; it is man *sub specie Christi* and not the reverse. Perhaps we find here the very core of the whole argument.

No wonder, then, that every discussion about the nature of Scripture, about its authority and validity as the word of God, appears to have its proper center and focus in the person and authority of Christ himself as he is presented and presents

himself to us in Scripture. No wonder, too, that in the recent
theological development the emphasis on the humanity of
Scripture is accompanied by interest in a new and radical
way in the humanity of Christ.

* * *

The emphasis on the true humanity of Jesus can be expressed
indeed in various ways. In the terminology of new theology
there is a certain preference for what is called Christology
"from below"; that means an approach to the person of Jesus
on the basis of his human appearance, as "the man of Nazareth." The church, as is well known, has developed a Christology "from above," speaking about Christ as the Son of
God and the second person of the divine Trinity. The question is whether the humanity of Jesus has been and can be
sufficiently respected in this latter formula.

Two recent Dutch theological studies, both of which have
attracted a great deal of attention, have approached Christology not "from above" but "from below." The well-known
Roman Catholic systematic theologian E. Schillebeeckx has
given his book the typical title *Jezus, het verhaal van een
levende* ("Jesus, the story of a living one"). It is presupposed
that each generation should have its own Christology on the
basis of the story of the historical Jesus. No doubt what the
church in the passing of time used to say about Jesus is important, but as a matter of fact this is not automatically understandable or acceptable to our generation. That also holds
true, according to Schillebeeckx, for the names and divine
qualities assigned to Jesus in the New Testament. These names
and qualities do express how the early church understood
Jesus as *Salvator* and how they defined and qualified the ultimate salvation in him. We have to do with the same Jesus.
But we would like to designate him in another way, on the
basis of our own confrontation with Jesus of Nazareth, our own
experience of his living Spirit, and our own concept of the
salvation of human life. For we are different people.

Inevitably this point of view raises the question whether the dogmatic approach to Jesus on the basis of his divinity does not take away the correct view of his humanity, indeed, does not make the true humanity of Jesus imaginary. Here the second of the two books I referred to, *Christian Faith,* by the Reformed theologian Hendrikus Berkhof, attracted no little attention with its argument that the doctrine of the eternal pre-existence of Christ cannot be brought into harmony with the true humanity of Jesus. The pre-existence of Jesus, Berkhof says, is a sort of later conclusion of the church. He speaks of an "ideal pre-existence": the man Jesus, in his words and deeds, in his death and resurrection (and Berkhof does not doubt this at all), so clearly shows signs of divinity that the church of the New Testament came to regard him as a pre-existent being descended from heaven, and designated him as such. Pre-existence in this perspective is thus not a qualification of the *being,* but of the *significance* of Jesus, as he proved himself during his lifetime and revealed himself after his resurrection.

It is clear that in the emphasis on the human and indirect character of revelation it is not only the divine nature of Scripture but also of Christ himself as the Son of God that is being challenged.

To be sure, this new approach to Christology cannot be faulted on the ground that it is "from below" and takes its point of departure in Jesus of Nazareth in his historical self-revelation rather than in the dogma of his divinity. For it is in this historical way — "from below," if you like — that Jesus is presented in the gospels themselves — at least in the first three. They do not start in heaven, with the second person of the Trinity, but on earth — Matthew in Nazareth, Luke in Bethlehem — and from there they go back — Matthew to Abraham and Luke (in the genealogy) to Adam.

Only in the fourth gospel is it different. There everything starts with the Word that was in the beginning with God. So perhaps we could say that in the fourth gospel not history, not the "historical" Jesus gets priority, but the dogma of the pre-existent Son of God. But the fourth gospel was the last written and its author was early referred to as the theologian. Therefore, with a view to Scripture, it cannot be wrong for the church in its proclamation before all things to preach Jesus as he appears to us in the gospel, in all his humanity and solidarity with people. He did not tread as a God over the earth: the Word became flesh and dwelt among us. This is what the author of the fourth gospel says also.

For that reason it is rightly said that God is a God of people, that he, in his salvation, directs himself to human life in all its depth and breadth. That also means that God and man are not competitors, as if God were everything and man nothing. Quite the contrary. What is at stake is human life. That is why he who was with God became man, a God of all people, of all races, but also of all generations, not only of ancient man but also of modern man. To that extent it is true that salvation continues to take on other forms and has different implications, must be "translated" and interpreted differently. That Jesus is the same yesterday, today, and forever cannot be claimed as a "conservative" slogan without acknowledgment of its "progressive" meaning. What it says is that Jesus Christ can never be overtaken by time, that he is never at a loss whatever changing times may bring. He leads his church into the future. The fact that he is the same, that he is the Lord of all peoples and generations, is not only because he is the Son of God, but no less because he was a man among men. The salvation of the world is deeply anchored in the incarnation of the word, yesterday, today, and in all eternity.

But if one ought not to object to this new development in Christology which takes as its starting point the historical self-revelation of Jesus of Nazareth, the real question remains: What is meant by this historical self-revelation? Is this the confrontation with Jesus Christ as he comes to us in the gospel? Or does this approach "from below" mean that Jesus of Nazareth is only to be understood as a man and nothing more — without a doubt a marvelous, incomprehensible man, but nevertheless to be placed within the boundaries of human life and possibilities? In the latter case everything in the gospels that exceeds this human limit cannot be the image of the historical Jesus himself. Instead, it is seen as the interpretation of faith of his followers, a *faith* we share with them, but whose explanation of his divine significance must be recognized as something they developed as persons of that era, using the concepts of their time. We may highly respect this interpretation, but it is nevertheless not decisive or authoritative for our conception and expression of faith in Jesus Christ.

It becomes obvious here how close the relation is between our faith in Holy Scripture and our faith in Jesus Christ. For the Christ of the Scriptures, for all his humanity, reveals an authority, a power, a consciousness of being sent by God and belonging to God, which breaks through the boundaries of humanness. This is true not only of the gospel of John, but also of the other gospels. The old idea that it is especially the gospel of Mark which means to give a "life of Jesus" in its human development only has long since been abandoned. All four gospels proclaim to us Jesus as the Christ in a way that exceeds the limits of human biography. Undoubtedly, they do it in different ways.

The question is not whether this difference is due to a different interpretation. The method of redaction criticism has proved this clearly. Decisive for what we are discussing is the question whether the proclamation of Jesus' divine authority, of his coming from God and his being God, in its different presentations, is merely an image created by the faith of his followers, or the witness of who Jesus really and truly *was*, in his words and deeds, in his death and resurrection.

And this is the way the Scriptures proclaim and declare him to us. They say: He was a man, he became flesh, he dwelt among us, but exactly for that reason — that he became man and was with us — we beheld his glory, the glory of the only begotten Son of the Father. Or to say it with the opening words of the first letter of John: "That which we have seen with our eyes, which we have looked upon and touched with our hands, concerning the word of life . . . we proclaim also to you." This is not only a witness of faith, but a witness of revelation. This is the real meaning of the word "witness" (*martyria*) in the Scriptures: life was revealed, and we have seen it and bear witness and proclaim unto you that eternal life, which has been with the Father and was manifested unto us. There is really no contradiction between faith and revelation here, but what finally counts in Scripture is not faith but revelation. One can say indeed that the Scriptures are a book of faith, but of a faith that rests on revelation and bears witness to that revelation. That is why the Scriptures are the Word of God *in* and *through* the word of man. And that is why in the attire of the Scriptures not only faith in Christ but also Christ himself comes to us.

Only in this way are the full secret, the power, the authority of the Scriptures unfolded to us. Only then do we understand that Jesus Christ was the man among men, yet not from man but *from God*. So we come back to the prologue of the gospel of John, to the doctrine of his divinity, not as a quality we have awarded him, not as an "ideal pre-existence," but as an acknowledgment of his glory, not only in the flesh, but, according to the revelation in the flesh, also of his glory before the world was. In this way Christology "from below" becomes also a Christology "from above," as is the case in the wonderful prologue of the fourth gospel.

* * *

Let us turn now to a third facet of contemporary developments in church and theology, the doctrine of the kingdom of God. The same trend we have seen twice in the preceding can also be noticed in this doctrine, specifically in the tremendous role that man is supposed to play in the revelation of the kingdom of God.

Until recently, under the influence of the theology of Karl Barth and others, every identification of the kingdom of God with human action was rejected as heresy. The kingdom of God, we were told, stands completely over against the world in which we live. The revelation of the kingdom does illumine our reality like a flash of lightning, but it does not coincide at all with human history and human society, not even with that of the church. The kingdom of God is entirely a matter of God's acting, and our involvement in it is only a matter of expecting, hoping, praying.

Today the climate of thinking about the kingdom of God is totally different: now it is conceived as a reality that enters human history, coincides with it in a certain sense, and moves history to its future fulfilment. That does not mean that God is no longer the subject of the coming of the kingdom. The idea is that the Lord God himself works in a horizontal way by means of man. Man is God's partner in the realization of the kingdom. Thus the kingdom is not to be sought above or behind or outside of human history, but where God and man work together in the opening of the future and the realization of a new and other world.

Closely connected to this general idea is the apparent concentration in recent theological development of everything on the social and political implications of the kingdom of God. Twenty or thirty years ago, in the heyday of existentialist interpretation, everything centered on individual man. Human history seemed to be no more than the entourage within which the individual existential confrontation with God has to take place. Now, however, things have changed radically in this respect — to the extent that the kingdom of God is seen to concern itself especially with the liberation of man in his involvement in the structures of society. Kingdom of God (so it is said) means above all a radical criticism of the dominant social and political powers in human life as the expression of human selfishness and oppressiveness on a worldwide scale. The kingdom of God does indeed mean the end of this world, but this end is not to be expected in an eschatological or apocalyptic way, as the end of human times and history, but rather as the transformation of or even violent revolution in the present structure of society by means of human intervention and human exertion. "Repent, for the kingdom of God is near" has to be understood as a radical criticism and call to conversion with respect to the acceptance of and the co-operation with the current powers and influences, which dominate human society.

This concept of the kingdom usually goes hand in hand with a fundamental criticism of the church. The church (so it is said time and again) is too much concerned with its own life and with personal salvation. As for God's kingdom in the whole world, the church contents itself with missionary work and saving souls. It is not in the center of the world, where the great problems of humanity are to be solved. Instead of being the great standard-bearer, carrying aloft the banner of justice and hope in this world, pleading the cause of the oppressed and the discriminated-against, the church adapts itself to the structures of this world as though these were not its business. At the same time, outside the church is where dissatisfaction with the existing order is taking radical shape, sometimes even displaying the impatience and power of a real messianic longing for a better world. Could it be that Christ himself is moving and working in the dissatisfaction and revolutions of the world more than in the institutions of church and Christianity? Would it therefore not be preferable for the church, instead of preserving its own identity so anxiously, to commit itself to every attempt for a better world, for more justice and peace, in this way bringing kingdom of God and history together, instead of making a separation between them?

This new approach to the idea of the kingdom of God — perhaps it is not as new as it seems — has stirred a lot of reflection and discussion about the relation of the kingdom of God to the history of the world. This reflection is in my opinion very urgent — indeed, necessary. It also requires a new and careful examination of the biblical message of reconciliation, into which we shall go in more detail in one of

the following chapters, limiting ourselves here to some
general remarks.

First it should not and cannot be denied that, according to
the Scriptures, man is involved in the coming of the kingdom
in a very essential way. When Jesus proclaims his kingdom:
"All authority in heaven and on earth has been given to me,"
in the same breath he instructs his disciples: "Go therefore
and make disciples of all nations" (Matt. 28:18-19). And Paul,
in the profound sayings in his letters to the Ephesians and the
Colossians about Christ as the head of all things, speaks in
the same context about the church as the body of Christ,
calling it the *pleroma*, the fulness of Christ who fills all in
all (Eph. 1:20-23). That means, in the first place, that the
church as the body of Christ and the people of God is involved in a special way in the dominion of Christ. She is his
pleroma — perhaps we may say, the concentration point of
his grace and dominion. But at the same time it is said
that the kingship of Christ does *not* coincide with the church.
For Christ is the head over *all* things, and the church is the
pleroma of him who *fills* all things in all respects. These two
aspects of the dominion of Christ must be related to one other.

Second, this dominion of Christ over the church is a
spiritual one, as is said in the words which form the central
theme of the epistle to the Colossians, that God "has delivered
us from the dominion of darkness and transferred us to the
kingdom of his beloved Son" (1:13). But this spiritual dominion does not limit itself to the inner life; rather, it goes forth
as a spiritual power into the whole life of man. Jesus himself
has proclaimed the kingdom in words and deeds, and he is
the one who fulfils *all* things in *all* respects. Therefore the
kingdom of God has a liberating power with reference to
all human relations, too. It has something to say about mar-
riage, about slavery, about social and economic relations insofar as the liberation of human life is concerned. Hence, man's
responsibility and activity is involved in the coming of the
kingdom, not with respect only to his own individual salvation
but with respect to all things.

In my opinion, at this point recent developments in theology do urge the church to reconsider its identity as the church of Jesus Christ in the midst of this world. It is not surprising nor without reason that under the influence of this new emphasis on human involvement in the coming of God's universal kingdom, more and more attention is concentrated on the function of the church as the medium of the kingdom in the world. The question is heard again and again: Are the structures of the church adapted sufficiently to this mediating function of the church in our time? The church is always getting a thorough sociological and psychological examination, and usually, in this respect, with a negative result.

I can imagine that many faithful members of the church are sick and tired of all this criticism constantly aimed at the church, often from people who do not excel in attending church nor in knowledge of what is really going on — or ever has gone on — in the churches. Nevertheless, the real answer with regard to this development of the doctrine of the kingdom cannot lie in defenses of the undeniable weakness and shortcomings of the church in respect of its function in human society. Rather, the question must be posed: Has the church not often lost the biblical understandings of the kingdom of God, and of its own identity and responsibility as the body and *pleroma* of him who is the Lord of all things? Has it not adapted itself too easily to the current structures and powers of human society, thus contenting itself with the spiritual and future character of human ·salvation?

Third, no matter how urgent and critical these questions are with respect to the true identity and responsibility of the churches in this world, at the same time one must be aware that this identity is in danger in more than one way. In the development of recent theology the revelation of the kingdom of God is often closely linked to all sorts of current criticism of human society, to political and social movements and ideologies insofar as they wage a battle for freedom, justice, and peace. What are the grounds for expecting the coming of the kingdom of God in what I would call such a synthetical way? Can the situation of our day be approached and judged in so positive and often even optimistic a mood, as far as the kingdom of God is concerned? Was there ever a time when even in the struggle of human beings for liberation and peace alienation from God was greater and the autonomy of man experienced and proclaimed more radically than today? Regardless of how the church has to concentrate on the universal character of the kingdom of God, it must at the same time be careful not to exchange its message for or identify it with that of human ideologies, whatever they claim to be able to do in favor of man's liberation.

Here are real temptations for the church, which resemble the vision of Jesus in the wilderness when all kingdoms of earth and their glory were offered to him. In a sense this was a real messianic prospect, but under those conditions, with utter concentration, Jesus answered, "Be gone, Satan!" The way in which Jesus was to obtain worldwide dominion was another one. It was only in the way of self-surrender, of reconciliation on the cross, that to him was given all power in heaven and on earth. So he is portrayed in Revelation 5 as the lamb standing as though it had been slain, to whom the Father rendered the scroll of history and the future.

It is only as the body of *this* Christ that the church has to keep reconsidering its place and calling in the world to be a church that clings to the cross of its Lord as the only way in which his kingdom has come already and is to be expected to fulfil all things in all respects. That means that the subject of the kingdom is not "we," but "he," and that our role is not just to achieve and to fulfil what once was started by God in his Son Jesus Christ. It was he who opened the way once and forever; it is also he who is continuing to fulfil all things by the power of his blood and Spirit. People are coming in as objects and as instruments of his redeeming dominion, just as and insofar as they share in his *pleroma*: that means as far as they live under his liberating kingship and are prepared to follow him in his compassion and self-surrender and to obey him in his commandments concerning the needs of the world. The most severe criticism of the church, then, is that made on the basis of its own identity as the body of Christ, at the same time providing it with the only possibility to be a light, a salt, a blessing for the world.

Perhaps in this so-called post-Christian era the role of the church, more than it often used to be, is like that of the early church, which had to find its way into the future in the midst of an immense world pressing in on it from all sides. This church from the outset is warned continually to preserve its identity as the church of Jesus Christ, being as such not against but in favor of this world. A passage from the letter of Jude has often come to my mind in recent discussions. "But you, beloved, build yourselves up on your most holy faith; pray in the Holy Spirit; keep yourselves in the love of God; wait for the mercy of our Lord Jesus Christ unto eternal life. And convince some, who doubt; save some, by snatching them out of the fire; on some have mercy with fear, hating even the garment spotted by the flesh" (Jude 20-23).

It is all here in this beautiful passage: "Keep yourselves" as the church, as the people of God. Do not abandon yourselves as a church, whatever people say about your self-preservation. But this is not the same thing as conservatism, because you have to keep yourself *in the love of God*. And that is something other than to stay with yourself or with your history. For the love of God is always new, enclosing the world and all its misery.

We are also taught here about *how* we can preserve ourselves in the love of God: not by resting, but by "building," renewing ourselves and our church on the once laid foundation of our most holy faith. Also by praying and expecting, living in the communion of the Lord who lives and accepting from his hands the way to the future with hope and expectation. On this way we are reminded to be merciful to those in the fire between belief and unbelief, between being under the dominion of the Lord and under the power of the world. We must have compassion, not condemning too much and too quickly, but aware, too, of the danger of being contaminated by the plague or leprosy, which clings sometimes even to the clothes of those who want to touch and embrace you, bringing you back into the slavery of darkness.

2.

The Inspiration and
Authority of Holy Scripture

WHEN SPEAKING ABOUT the authority of the Scriptures, one must distinguish sharply from the beginning between this authority itself and our *doctrine about* Scripture, its authority, infallibility, and all qualifications and concepts concerning Holy Scripture that have proceeded from theological reflection and discussion over the years. The Bible itself gives no systematic doctrine of its attributes, of the relationship in it of the divine and human. Its point of view is other than that of theology.

This does not mean, of course, that the Bible has nothing to say about its authority and infallibility. The authority of the Scriptures is the great presupposition of the whole of the biblical preaching and doctrine. This appears most clearly in the way the New Testament speaks about the Old Testament. That which appears in the Old Testament is cited in the New Testament with formulas like "God says," "the Holy Spirit says," and so on (cf., for instance, Acts 3:24, 25; 2 Cor. 6:16; Acts 1:16). What "the Scripture says" and what "God says" is the same thing. The Scripture may be personified, as if it were God himself (Gal. 3:8; Rom. 9:17). This "indicates a certain confusion in current speech between 'Scripture' and 'God,' the outgrowth of a deep-seated conviction that the word of Scripture is the Word of God. It was not 'Scripture' that spoke to Pharaoh (Rom. 9:17), or gave his great promise to Abraham (Gal. 3:8), but God. But 'Scripture' and 'God' lay so close together in the minds of the writers of the New Testament that they could naturally speak of 'Scripture' doing

20

what Scripture records God as doing" (B. B. Warfield). And this naturally implies *authority.* "It is written" (Greek, *gegraptai*) in the New Testament puts an end to all contradiction.

This authority of the Scriptures of the Old Testament is no other than that which the apostles ascribe to themselves, namely as heralds, witnesses, ambassadors of God and Christ (Rom. 1:1,5; 1 Tim. 2:7; Gal. 1:8,9; 1 Thess. 2:13). They attach that authority in the same manner to their writings as to their words (1 Cor. 15:1f.; 2 Thess. 2:15; 3:14). In the New Testament the apostolic writings are already placed on a par with those of the Old Testament (2 Pet. 3:15,16; Rev. 1:3). *Gegraptai* is already used of the writings of the New Testament (John 20:31). And the New Testament concept of faith is in accord with that: it is *obedience* to the apostolic witness (Rom. 1:5; 16:26; 10:3). This apostolic witness is fundamentally distinguished in this respect from other manifestations of the Spirit, which demand of the congregation (*ekklesia*) not only obedience, but also a critical discernment between the true and the false (cf. 1 Thess. 5:21; 1 John 4:1). For this witness deserves unconditional faith and obedience, in its written as well as in its oral form.

Similarly for infallibility. Although, as far as I am aware, the equivalent of our word "infallibility" as attribute of the Scripture is not found in biblical terminology, yet in agreement with Scripture's divine origin and content, great emphasis is repeatedly placed on its *trustworthiness.* The prophetic word is sure (*bebaios*) (2 Pet. 1:19). In the Pastoral Epistles Paul does not tire of assuring his readers that the word he has handed down is trustworthy (*pistos*) and worthy of full acceptance (1 Tim. 1:15; 3:1; 4:9; 2 Tim. 2:11; Titus 3:8). In Hebrews 2:3 the author writes that salvation was declared at first by the Lord and it was attested (made *bebaios*) to us by those who heard him. While it must be said of man that "all flesh is grass," it is true of the word of God that "it abides forever." And "that word is the good news, *which was preached to you*" (1 Pet. 1:24,25).

The abiding and trustworthy word of God has thus entered into the spoken and written word of the apostles. As Luke tells Theophilus, the tradition of what was heard and seen by those who were from the beginning eyewitnesses and ministers of the word has been written down so that he might recognize the trustworthiness (*asphaleia*) of that of which he has been informed (Luke 1:1-4). The whole of Scripture is full of declarations that the one who builds on the word and promise of God will not be ashamed (Isa. 28:16; Rom. 9:33; 1 Pet. 2:6); this applies to the spoken as well as to the written word of the apostles (John 19:35; 20:31; 1 John 1:1-3). The Scripture is infallible, so we may summarize, because it does not fail, because it has the significance of a foundation on which the *ekklesia* has been established and on which it must increasingly establish itself (Col. 2:6,7). The whole concept of *tradition,* as it is used by Paul, for example, has this connotation of authority, certainty, irrefutability. Protestants thus do well not to give up this concept out of reaction against its use in Roman Catholicism. The authority and infallibility of the Scriptures are thus two sides of the same coin: namely, that the Scripture is of God.

The second thing we have to observe from the beginning is that all attributes which the Scripture ascribes to itself stand in close relationship to its purpose and nature. And so our way of thinking about Scripture and our theological definitions must also be related to this purpose.

It is obvious that Scripture is given us for a definite purpose. Paul says that it "was written for our instruction, that by steadfastness and by the encouragement of the scriptures we might have hope" (Rom. 15:4). The famous pronouncement of 2 Timothy 3:15-16 is to the same effect: the sacred writings "are able to instruct you for salvation through faith in Christ Jesus." Not only is the nature and force of the Scriptures to be found in their providing instruction for salvation, so is the means and key for understanding them — faith in Jesus Christ. Only by the light of such faith is the treasure of wisdom and knowledge of the Scriptures unlocked.

This purpose of Scripture (of the Old Testament as well as the New) and the use which corresponds to it must always be borne in mind when framing a theological definition of the attributes of the Scripture. That is the thrust of Calvin's comment on 2 Timothy 3:15: "In order that it may be profitable to salvation to us, we have to learn to make right use of it. . . . He has good reason to recall us to the faith of Christ, which is the center and sum of Scripture." What follows in verse 16 is in complete accord with this: "All Scripture is inspired by God" — and the predicative significance of *theopneustos* is not in my opinion disputable — "and profitable for teaching, for reproof, for correction and for training in righteousness." The purpose and the nature of Scripture lie thus in that qualified sort of teaching and instruction which is able to make us wise to salvation, which gives God's people this "completeness" and equips them for every good work.

That we cannot speak about Scripture and its qualities apart from this scope, purpose, and nature, should also be the point of departure of every theological evaluation and definition of biblical authority. This authority is not to be separated from the content and purpose of Scripture thus qualified nor can it be recognized apart from this content and the specific character of the Scripture. No matter to what extent we reject the dualistic doctrine of inspiration, which holds that only the religious-ethical sections of Scripture are inspired and authoritative, this does not remove the fact that, in Herman Bavinck's words, "Holy Scripture has a thoroughly religious-ethical purpose (designation, intention) and is not intended to be a handbook for the various sciences." We may not apply to the Scripture standards which do not suit it. Not only does it give no exact knowledge of mathematics or biology, but it also presents no history of Israel or biography of Jesus that accords with the standards of historical science. Therefore, one must not transfer biblical authority.

God speaks to us through the Scriptures not in order to make us scholars, but to make us Christians. To be sure, to make us Christians in our science, too, but not in such a way as to make human science superfluous or to teach us in a supernatural way all sorts of things that could and would otherwise be learned by scientific training and research.

What Scripture does intend is to place us as humans in a right position to God, even in our scientific studies and efforts. Scripture is not concerned only with persons' *religious* needs in a pietistic or existentialistic sense of that word. On the contrary, its purpose and authority is that it teaches us to understand everything *sub specie Dei* — humanity, the world, nature, history, their origin and their destination, their past and their future. Therefore the Bible is not only the book of conversion, but also the book of history and the book of creation. But it is the book of history of salvation; and it is this point of view that represents and defines the authority of Scripture.

But when one connects the theological definition of authority and infallibility as attributes of Scripture so closely with Scripture's purpose and nature, does one not run the danger of falling into a kind of subjectivism? Who will establish precisely the boundaries between that which does and that which does not pertain to the purpose of the Scripture? And is the way not thus opened for subjectivism and arbitrariness in the matter of the authority of the Scripture, as has been so detrimental to the authority of the Scripture in the history of the church? I should like in this connection to point out the following:

First, the misuse of the Scripture does not abolish the good and correct use. A Scripture is not a book of separate divine oracles, but is from Genesis to Revelation an organic unity, insofar as it is the book of the history of God's redeeming and judging acts, of which the advent and work of Christ is the all-dominating center and focus. The testimony of Jesus is the spirit of prophecy (Rev. 19:10), and Scripture has the power to save by faith in Christ Jesus (2 Tim. 3:15). This is the center to which everything in Scripture stands in relationship and through which it is bound together — beginning and end, creation and re-creation, humanity, the world, history, and the future, as all of these have a place in the Scripture. Therefore, there is also a correlation between Scripture and faith, namely, as faith in Jesus Christ. If you take that unity away from Scripture and this correlation of Scripture and faith, you denature Scripture and faith in it; and the authority and infallibility of the Scripture also lose their theological-christological definition and become formal concepts, abstracted from the peculiar nature and content of Scripture.

But in the second place, that does not mean we are permitted to apply all sorts of dualistic operations on Scripture and make distinctions between what is and what is not inspired, what is and what is not from God — to say, for instance, that the content but not the form, or the essence but not the word was subject to the might and inspiration and authority of God. God gave us the Scripture in this concrete form, in these words and languages. The confession applies to this, and not to specific sections or thoughts, that it is the inspired word of God, that it is given to us as the infallible guide to life, God's light on our path, God's lamp for our feet. But divine inspiration does not necessarily mean that the men who spoke and wrote under inspiration were temporarily stripped of their limitations in knowledge, memory, language, and capability of expressing themselves, as specific human beings in a certain period of history.

We have to be very careful, I think, not to operate as though we know ahead of time to what extent divine inspiration does or does not go together with the human limitations mentioned above. Inspiration does not mean deification. We cannot say everything of Scripture that we say of the word of God, nor can we identify the apostles and prophets during their writing with the Holy Spirit. The Word of God exists in eternity, is perfect. But Scripture is neither eternal nor perfect. Inspiration consists in this, that God makes the words of men the instrument of his word, that he uses human words for his divine purposes. As such the human words stand in the service of God and participate in the authority and infallibility of the Word of God, answer perfectly God's purpose, in short, function as the Word of God and therefore can be so called. But this remains a human instrument in the hands of God. And it is not up to us, it is up to the free pleasure of God to decide what kind of effect divine inspiration should have in the mind, knowledge, memory, accuracy of those whom he has used in his service, in order that their word really can be accepted and trusted as the inspired word of God. If we deny or ignore this, we dispose of the very nature of the Scriptures as the Word of God, and also of the nature of his authority and infallibility. The best way not to fall into such a danger is to study Scripture itself from this point of view.

*   *   *

In order not to get bogged down in generalities and abstractions I will demonstrate what I mean with a number of examples from the Bible itself.

One of the proofs that the authority and infallibility of Scripture are to be understood in a qualified sense is the way the synoptic gospels present the same material with several different arrangements, sequences, and expressions. Undoubtedly the total picture that these evangelists draw of Jesus is entirely the same, not only in its totality but also in many details. Therefore, when we read the gospels one after another (in the manner and with the intention with which the church may and must read them) nobody will have for even an instant the impression that the Christ of the one gospel is a different one in comparison with the image of Christ in another gospel.

Yet this does not mean that there are no differences in historical details, or in the tendency of two or three evangelists' telling the same story, or in the reproduction of the same words and deeds of Jesus, or in the presentation and interpretation of the good news as a whole. Nor are those differences limited to little details, which one can easily neglect or dismiss. Compare, for instance, the Lord's Prayer in Mat-

thew and Luke. It is apparent that Luke, in addition to recording a shorter address of God, lacks the third petition entirely and for the last petition has only: "Lead us not into
temptation."

Now, one might suggest that Jesus gave his disciples the
Lord's Prayer on two different occasions in two different
formulations, thus tracing differences between Matthew and
Luke back to Jesus himself and not to the recording of the
evangelists. No one can prove that this is impossible. But it
is quite another thing to assert that Jesus himself *must* have
given the Lord's Prayer twice, in two different forms; or that
otherwise the inspiration and infallibility of Scripture have
failed. One must be able to realize that on one and the same
occasion spoken words of Jesus were recorded in different
ways and that often it cannot possibly be established which
is the historically exact reproduction. For even if you hesitate
about whether the Lord's Prayer was given on one or two
occasions (a matter, Calvin says, "about which I will be at odds
with no one"), nevertheless, you cannot do this with regard
to certain other words of Jesus. The beatitudes of Matthew
differ considerably from those of Luke, although surely no
one any longer would be willing to accept two Sermons on the
Mount. And the record of the institution of the Lord's supper,
while in the substance of the matter much the same, displays,
in the tradition of Matthew and Mark on the one side and that
of Luke and Paul on the other, various more or less interesting and important differences.

All this has yet nothing to do with *essential* trustworthiness
or infallibility. For the gospels, as the basis on which Christ
builds his *ekklesia,* all these differences in tradition regarding
the Lord's Prayer, the Beatitudes, the words of the Lord's supper, constitute no problem. But if one attempts to design a doctrine concerning Holy Scripture, he must surely not lose sight
of this freedom and difference of presentation. One cannot
postulate on the basis that the books of the New Testament are
God-breathed that "every word then must precisely reproduce
the historical situation, for otherwise the Scripture would not

be 'infallible.' " The fact is that the infallibility of Scripture has in many respects a character other than that which a theoretical concept of inspiration or infallibility, detached from its purpose and empirical reality, would like to demand. One must be careful when reasoning about what is and what is not possible under inspiration by God. Here too the freedom of the Spirit must be honored; and we shall first have to trace the courses of the Spirit in reverence, rather than come at once to overconfident pronouncements, however proper our intentions.

To mention another, slightly different example which casts light on this so-called organic character: we see occasionally that one evangelist purposely introduces changes into what another has written, sometimes, apparently, in order to correct him. Though there is no absolute certainty about the mutual relationship of Matthew, Mark, and Luke, there is a probability bordering on certainty that Mark was the first to write his gospel and that Matthew and Luke constructed theirs on the basis of Mark's. In Matthew, in any case, we observe a clear systematizing of material which in Mark lies scattered far apart. This indicates a different design and development of common material. It does not necessarily imply that the one is "better" than the other, but does indeed point again to the elbow-room allowed the evangelists in their presentation of the same message.

Occasionally, this leads to remarkable results. In the story of the rich young ruler Jesus says, according to Mark 10:18, "Why do you call me good? No one is good but God alone." In Matthew 19:17, however, we read the same material (from Mark) this way: "Why do you ask me about what is good? One there is who is good." It is possible that there are two traditions here, but one must also take into account the possibility that Matthew expressed in somewhat different words the material used by Mark to avoid the implication that Jesus should not have considered himself "good." This is not to say that Mark indeed meant that, only that Matthew wished to safeguard against a misunderstanding of the version which we meet in Mark.

This remarkable difference between the two furnishes no difficulty whatever for the essential authority of the gospel, but it does enable us to see that a doctrine of "verbal inspiration" which aims at closing off discussion of the historical precision and accuracy of every word in the Bible is exceeding its area of competence. That is not to say that therefore there is inspiration only in respect of the matter and not the word: such a distinction is much too mechanical. But it is indeed to say that inspiration is something other than an elimination of human freedom and human limitation. The Spirit certainly takes care that the church not suffer deficiency and that it may believe and preach on the basis of the *written* word. But the way down which the Spirit travels and the liberty he grants himself and the writers of the Bible are not capable of being expressed in one neat dogmatic formula. It is the liberty of the Spirit; we must approach it with respect and discuss it in our theological statements with caution.

That we must not form an abstract theological concept of the inspiration and authority of the Scripture, but instead pay heed to how the writers of the Bible went about their work, also appears from another phenomenon that strikes us again and again in the study of the Bible. Although the biblical writers were equipped by the Holy Spirit for the task they had to fulfil in the service of God's special revelation for all times and generations, they were nevertheless in many respects entirely children of their own time; and to this extent they thought and wrote and narrated just as their contemporaries thought and wrote and narrated. This is true not only of the languages in which they wrote, which have become dead languages, but also of their concepts, their ideas, their manner of expression, their methods of communication. All these were in a sense conditioned in various ways by the time and milieu in which they lived. And it cannot be said of all these concepts and ideas that, because they have received a place in the

Bible, they have also received the significance of infallible revelation.

However difficult — even dangerous — it may be to operate with this form-content schema, no one must be under the illusion that he can avoid it in the theological exegesis and explanation of the message of the Bible. Everything depends on how and why such a schema is used. Whenever it is used in the service of a naturalistic and evolutionary world-view, it is a destructive instrument, a dissecting knife, which cuts the Scripture off from the roots that give it life and makes it just another remnant of the ancient Near Eastern or hellenistic spirit. More than once it has been treated precisely that way; so it is no wonder that the evangelical view of Scripture listens with extreme suspicion, raised eyebrows, and heightened vigilance when modern scholars apply this form-content schema, these accommodation-theories, to the Bible.

But there is another side to the matter. From the standpoint of faith, the nature of the Scripture and its authority can surely be more sharply, clearly, and precisely distinguished when we see the Bible against the background and in the light of the time in which it was written. Then we come to see on the one hand the incomparable otherness of Scripture, and on the other that which is bound up with and limited to the time.

In this connection mention is often made of the influence the ancient Near Eastern conception of the universe had on how the biblical writers thought and expressed themselves. Some have wanted to deny this influence by saying that these authors spoke of such things just as we do in everyday life when we speak of "sunrise" and the like. But it is surely difficult to maintain this. If there are said to be three stories in the universe, as for example in Exodus 20 and still in Philippians 2 (heaven, earth, and that which is under the earth), this is positively not a scientific, but still a traditional, generally current representation of the structure of the universe. We can hardly think in such terms anymore. We can no longer think so "massively" of heaven and so spatially of the ascension as was possible in the representations of the biblical writers. It is clear that the "translation" of *this* confronts us with much greater problems than does the translation of the Old and New Testaments into a modern language, but this does not take away the fact that in this respect the Scripture speaks in images and concepts, exhibiting the stamp and also the relativity of the time in which they were current.

In another respect, too, it is clear that the writers of the Bible associated themselves with what, by virtue of education or tradition, pertained to the manner of speaking and thinking of their contemporaries, without enabling one thus to say that since this or that idea or expression finds a place in the Bible, it thereby becomes "revelation." This is the more obvious because the content of the Bible doubtless signals a radical breakthrough into all sorts of contemporary convictions and traditions. To take one prominent example, Paul's preaching is a continuous antithesis to the Jewish synagogical schema of redemption. In this fundamental sense Paul is the apostle of Christ and one inspired by the Spirit. But this does not remove the fact that this same apostle still betrays some traces of his rabbinical education, for example in the manner in which he debates, uses rabbinical argumentation and traditional materials, cites the Old Testament.

Certainly even in this "formal" sense the difference between Paul and the synagogue is greater than the conformity between them; and the message of Christ signifies in his disciples, too, a clearing away and purging of all kinds of subtle and casuistical rabbinical lore. But in some respects the Jewishness and the rabbinical background of New Testament writings are clear enough. If the second letter to Timothy speaks of Jannes and Jambres as men who withstood Moses, we cannot recognize in them the Egyptian magicians of the court of Pharaoh, until we come across these same names in certain late Jewish writings with a plain reference to those magicians. Elsewhere, when Paul speaks of the mediation of angels in giving the law on Sinai (Gal. 3:19), or when, wishing to indicate Christ's exaltation above all other spiritual powers, he lists a whole series of kinds of angels (Col. 1:16); or says that the promise was given 430 years before the law (Gal. 3:17) — these are all expressions whose background we are not able to find in the Old Testament or elsewhere in the New Testament, but which only become clear to us from the late Jewish writings. How must we now view this? Must we say that because Paul, the apostle of Christ, who was led by the Spirit, calls the magicians of Pharaoh Jannes and Jambres, these must have been their real names? Although there may have been those in times past who would have answered this affirmatively, it would not be easy to mention anyone who takes this standpoint today, at least among those aware of the way these names were probably brought into vogue in Jewish literature.

Now, of course, the concrete significance of this last example is particularly slight. From the point of view of faith no one is interested in the names of Pharaoh's magicians. Nevertheless, as an example, this case of Jannes and Jambres is not without importance. It lets us see that inspiration can also mean connection with certain Jewish or non-Christian elements, without these elements at the same time being brought under the sanction of inspiration and thus belonging to the normative character of the Scripture.

More is at stake here than a name or a number, as anyone realizes who has been confronted by these things in his investigation of the Scripture. The non-scholarly reader of the Bible can understand this, too. This has to do with literary genres, with methods of writing history, with the sometimes fluid boundaries of a parabolic narrative and a historical narrative. When in the book of Job a marvelous dialogue between Job and his friends is presented in artistic language, everyone can grasp that this is not a stenographic transcription of a number of improvised speeches which an afflicted man and his friends, who had been sitting in ashes silently for seven days and nights, uttered one after another; but rather that here the problem of theodicy, of "justifying God's ways to man," is posed and treated in a dramatic fashion. And when Matthew's genealogy of Jesus is formulated in a series of three sets of fourteen names, one can by comparing this with the data of the Old Testament, which include more names in the same line of descent, come to no other conclusion than that the evangelist has either deliberately "stylized" this himself or has used an already existing stylizing. It will not do to say, "It does not tally," or something like that. One must come to appreciate that there is a difference beween our exact Western spirit and the spirit of someone two thousand years ago who, in other circumstances and with other objects in view, recorded his vision of history.

In this same genealogy of Matthew there are more proofs of this. However, our concern here is not with further details but with an overall approach to these things which does as much justice as possible to the particular nature of Scripture and its authority. In this approach we must always be aware that we are dealing with the Scripture as the Word of God. So, it would be a denial of the very nature of Scripture if, in view of what we have been discussing here, we were to acknowledge Scripture as only a human attempt to give expression to and interpretation of what some human writers long ago might, by way of their belief, have understood of the word of God; and, in addition, we would consider that our engagement to the Bible would consist only in having to do the same thing as they did: staying in the line of their tradition and passing on what they understood of the word of God, in our language, way of thinking, and by our means of interpretation.

I say this would be a perversion of the nature of Scripture. For what we are confronted with in Scripture is not just human beings in their human faith and human efforts to witness to what they understood of God's revelation; it is God *himself,* addressing himself to us by men. This is a real and essential difference, for it is the difference of the real subject and author of Scripture. But at the same time we must always be aware that it is God's speaking in his condescension to men, wonderfully adjusting himself to human language and human possibilities of understanding. Therefore what is presented to us in Scripture will always be a matter for listening to in submission to God's divine authority. It may never become a matter of "one's own interpretation" (new in every age), because no prophecy ever came by the impulse of man, but men moved by the Holy Spirit spoke from God (2 Pet. 1:20, 21). And at the same time listening to Scripture is listening to a human language, human concepts, human images, which we have to translate, in more than one respect, in order to understand what God is saying to us in and by means of Scripture.

* * *

Let us try to come to a conclusion.

To attempt a theological definition of the Scripture is no easy matter. This results from its unique origin and character. All Scripture is God-breathed. Therefore all our human definitions will remain inadequate. Just because it is divine, it arises above our knowledge, and we shall never fully realize "what is the breadth and length and height and depth" (Eph. 3:18). This applies also to its authority and infallibility. Its authority is much greater than we are able to express in human words. But at the same time we have to acknowledge that this Word of God has entered so very much into the human and has so identified itself with it that we shall always again stand before the question as to what the unassailably divine and what the relativity of the human in Scripture mean concretely. We stand before a very deep and mysterious task, transferring thoughts from the life and the world of persons of two thousand years ago and more to the world of today. Here lies the great question of hermeneutics, with which many today are engaged very intensively.

Nevertheless, it remains true that Scripture and its authority, in the most profound and central sense of the word, is not obscure but clear, namely, in the manner in which it teaches persons to understand themselves, the world, history, and the future in the light of the God and Father of Jesus Christ. It

is on account of this clarity of the Scripture that it is an ever-
flowing well of knowledge and life and that it teaches wisdom
to the simple. And it is on account of this clarity and this
purpose of the Scripture that it can be identified with the
Word of God, that it has unconditional authority, and that it
is the infallible foundation for faith.

Finally I should like to say a couple things in reponse to the
claim that the intricate way theology speaks about the authority and infallibility of the Scripture lacks the power and sim-
plicity of a less complicated, more "naive" approach. First, when
new light is cast on the Scripture, also through the investi-
gations of historical science, the church has to rejoice, even
though this may compel it at the same time to be ready to
reconsider and redefine theological concepts related to
Scripture.

In the second place, remember that just those who have
occasion to come to a more historical approach to the Bible
and its authority will be able along the way to understand
the unique and incomparable significance of Scripture. The
world of the ancient Near East is being increasingly opened to
us. We are discovering very ancient "literature" in which the
religious feelings of people who were contemporaries of the
biblical writers are expressed. There is increasing Jewish
background through the Talmud and through insights into
the radical movements in the Judaism of Jesus' time through
the discovery of the Qumran writings. Of more recent date
still is the discovery in Egypt of an entire library of gnostic
literature from the second century.

All of this teaches us more strongly than ever to be mindful of
the relationship between Scripture and the world out of which
it arose. At once we see a striking establishment of the historical correctness of the biblical data and then again are placed
before questions in which we cannot always see a priori that
"the Bible is right." But something else is far more important:
namely, that there is nothing that more clearly brings to the
light the unique character of the Scriptures than the qualitative
comparison between that which here and that which there

steps out to meet us. That difference does not lie in a more advanced human development, or greater accuracy, or another manner of tradition. It inheres in what we have again and again described as the purpose and the qualitative content of the Scripture. On the one side we find legalistic scrupulousness, flight into the speculative, invincible fear of death. On the other side, in the Scriptures of the Old and New Testaments, we see a qualitatively different knowledge of God and of nature, faith in forgiveness, the conquest of death, dying with Christ to that which Paul describes as the weak and poor principles of the world.

The difference is not easy to put into words. The expression in one of the Reformation confessions from the sixteenth century is not too strong or too naive: the Scriptures "carry the evidence in themselves" of their divinity and authority (Belgic Confession, Art. V). For where the testimony of Christ appears, there not only does the light arise, but also the darkness is illuminated; as it is said of Jesus, he spoke with authority and not as the scribes did. This is not to imply that the *doctrine concerning* the Holy Scriptures has become a simple matter. But in the light of *this* authority, we can overcome the fear that we may be on a dangerous pathway if we view the ways of the Spirit in recording the word of God more historically, more critically, as more shaded, than along the way of an exclusively dogmatic reasoning.

We shall come to stand before more questions, perhaps before more questions without answers. That is the lot of everyone who will gather science to himself: he gathers grief, too. But at the same time, the light that shines in the darkness is so clear and so bright that not only the prophet but even the far more skeptical theologian has to confess: "I have seen a limit to all perfection, but thy commandment is exceedingly broad" (Ps. 119:96).

3.

The Character of Research into the Synoptic Gospels

THE HISTORY of the research of the synoptic gospels has gone through several phases displaying different points of departure. Let us look in this chapter at a number of these.

a. *The gospels are originally separate units written by the apostles or their helpers to give to the later early church a kind of biography of Jesus.*

This is still the most popular approach. Its great merit is that it takes its point of departure in the historical character of the gospels and the tradition concerning the words, deeds, death, and resurrection of Jesus. That was of course the aim of the gospel writers — to give an image of the historical Jesus as an answer to the question: Who was he? One can still differ about whether there was any special reason for the gospels to be written. They originated relatively late: thirty to fifty years after the death of Jesus.

One can suppose that over a period of time the image of Jesus had become somewhat vague, thus creating the danger of an exclusively spiritual (even spiritualistic) conception of the Christian faith (docetism), making it necessary to rebuild a clear image of the "historical" Jesus. But I think one can with equal justification regard the gospels as the written formulation of the already existing narrative of Jesus, because of the important role that it played in the early church. In both instances, however, the concern is with the knowledge of the earthly or historical Jesus. Nevertheless, scholarly investigation has shown that it is improper to speak of a "biography" in the accepted sense of the word. That the gospels do not give unified orderly images of the historical unfolding of events needs little elaboration. Geographically, for example, the travels of Jesus cannot be reconstructed. Was he primarily in Galilee, as the synoptics indicate, or did he transfer his ministry time and again to Jerusalem, as suggested by the fourth gospel? The synoptics give us no direct information, merely a few indirect allusions (Luke 10:38; Matt. 23:37). The same holds true for the length of Jesus' public ministry. His age, his youth, his outward appearance, his inner life are in many respects unknown to us.

As a consequence, the gospels as historical books were subjected to severe criticism. If you accept historical biography as a criterion, you are bound to conclude that the gospel writers were relatively incompetent. Either they were badly informed about the real state of affairs or they were totally uninterested in it. This criticism was concerned primarily with the historical "gaps" in the image of Jesus delineated with the literary irregularities and obscurities in the transition from one narrative to the next, and with all kinds of inconsistencies and differences in presentation between and among the various gospels. As a result the gospels began to be viewed as the end-product of earlier (or older) sources, oral and written, of which the writers made use in a rather clumsy and arbitrary way.

This literary-critical approach thus became entangled in a large number of source-hypotheses, in which each hypothesis was even more complicated than its predecessor. Ultimately, the only definite result was that Matthew and Luke were more or less dependent on Mark (or an Ur-Markus), and that they showed traces of a common *logia*-source — the well-known "two-sources hypothesis." It can hardly be denied that some greater clarity about the mutual relationships of the synoptics was obtained in this way, but the proponents of the literary-historical method did not even come close to a consensus about the specific character of the gospels as historical books.

b. *The literary-historical method was succeeded by the form-critical method.*

The form-critical viewed the gospels in a completely different way. It did not see in them original units, nor did it view them as biographies; rather, it chose to see them as a collection of traditions found in the early church. The gospels are simply a framework in which all sorts of traditions were brought together.

The gospel writers were not independent historians, on this view, but editors or compilers. Thus the genre "gospel" becomes a secondary issue. It is more important to try to trace the various smaller units from which the gospels were composed. The form-critical method thus distinguishes in the words of Jesus between prophetic words, wisdom words, law words, "I" (ego-)utterances, parables, and so on; and in the deeds of Jesus, the fixed and often recurring forms of miracle-stories, "short-stories," and the like. Having done that, it then tries to trace *how* and *where* these various forms of tradition functioned — for example, in preaching, catechizing, or mission work among Gentiles or non-Christians.

Conversely, this *Sitz im Leben* can offer an explanation not only of the form of the tradition but also of the way the content of the tradition received its special shape; that is, how it has been re-created or even created. The tradition is understood to have been influenced in all sorts of ways by the experiences or the circumstances in which the early church lived, by the Jewish as well as by the pagan milieu, by the problems within the church itself, and by the variety of convictions that lived side by side within the church.

For this reason, some representatives of the form-critical method do not consider the synoptics a witness primarily about Jesus but rather about the faith of the early church, about the way it confessed or believed in Jesus. The gospels are not biography but kerygma, specifically kerygma influenced by the pluriformity which played within the Jewish-Christian, pagan-Christian church in the fifty years after Jesus' death. The advantage of the form-critical method is that it attempts to penetrate into the history of the synoptic tradition and gives us a clearer insight into the character of this tradition. It has correctly asserted that the motive behind this tradition was not simple interest in pure history — an effort to learn as much as possible about the life of Jesus and to transmit it faithfully — but to make converts to Jesus and establish them in the faith. In other words, the history of Jesus is not communicated in an objective-historical way, but betrays a tendency that can be called kerygmatic. That tendency has had a selective impact on the traditions and a formative influence on how these traditions were presented.

This was itself no new insight. The well-known citation of Papias about the gospel of Mark (in Eusebius, *Church History*, III.39) had already observed that not everything in the gospels was narrated in historical-chronological order, but in accordance with the requirements made by the preaching and teaching. For Mark himself was not an eyewitness, but merely the interpreter of Peter, as Papias notes. And Peter composed his teachings with special regard to the requirements of his listeners, not with the primary intent of giving a summary of the words and deeds of Jesus.

But this correct view of the character of the synoptic tradition is dominated to no little extent by the radical historical skepticism of many of the representatives of the form-critical method (especially the dean of that school Rudolf Bultmann), which leads them to question the historical truthworthiness of the tradition. So completely has the tradition become kerygma to them, that is, a summons to faith and decision, that for them the historical nature of the tradition plays only the most subordinate role. History disappears behind the kerygma. The real question when investigating the synoptics is not: Who was Jesus?, but Who did Jesus become to the early church? What is the actual, existential decision to which the gospel intends to urge us? The early church does not give us the image of the historical Jesus but the expression of its faith in the risen Lord, and this faith is projected back into the stories and words of the historical Jesus. Therefore, the early church is not only the *Sitz im Leben* of the tradition in her form-giving and development, but also its genesis, its origin, its source.

The form-critical method *by itself* does not lead to this destructive criticism of the historical reliability of the synoptic tradition. No two representatives of this method agree as to the reliability of the gospels. This is not the result of what the method can prove on scientific grounds, but basically depends on the presuppositions of those who use this method. To many of them it makes little difference how much or how little in the gospels can be accepted as history, since (so these scholars say) the synoptic tradition is concerned with kerygma and not with history. Still, as true as it is that the gospels are not biographies with only historical interest, it cannot be denied that they attempt to establish the faith of the early church on the story of the historical Jesus. In other words, to play kerygma off against history short-changes the character of the synoptic tradition.

This insight has happily emerged anew in the most recent literature. For instance, Graham Stanton contends in an essay in a 1972 collection entitled *Christ, Faith and History* that the oft-repeated dictum "the gospels are not biographies" needs careful reappraisal. Of course it is true that the gospels are not to be read against the background of modern biographical writings. But when we compare them with contemporary biographies, it appears that the presentations of the life of Jesus in the gospels are much less distinctive than usually is believed (p. 197). It is certainly true that the church retained no tradition about Jesus *solely* out of historical interest or biographical curiosity, for the traditions are kerygmatic and were used in the service of the preaching of the primitive church. But what is commonly suggested as a corollary to this — that since the gospel traditions are kerygmatic they are neither "historical" nor "biographical" in their perspective — is untenable: the kerygmatic role of the gospel traditions has not smothered interest in the life and character of Jesus. The dual perspective of the gospel traditions is inescapable: they intend to proclaim Jesus, they are also concerned with his life and character.

I think this judgment is correct. Why else would stories about Jesus have been written down in such detail and with such great care so long after his death, if concern was exclusively with the exalted Lord and not Jesus of Nazareth? The gospel of Jesus Christ, as Mark 1:1 summarizes the content of the whole book — that is to say, the story of the historical Jesus as good news — has guided the early church since the beginning of its existence as the basis of its faith (cf. Luke 1:1-4). The early church did not create the story; the story created the early church!

This does not deny but presupposes that the story was not only concerned with historical interest but was directed to the faith of the church. Influenced in many ways, it was selectively sorted and put in a special form. Nor does this view deny that the story was narrated and proclaimed in the light of the glorious resurrection of Christ. Without the resurrection the story would have lost its power. It would have been the story of the life of a saint, not the gospel. But the converse is also true: to know who the risen one *is*, to be able to believe in the resurrection, one has to know who Jesus *was*, one has to know the story of the earthly Jesus. And this is the way the story is presented: "that you may know the truth concerning the *things* of which you have been informed" (Luke 1:4; cf. John 20:31).

The interrelationship between kerygma and history is therefore unassailable; but it was the history that brought forth the kerygma, and this sequence cannot be reversed without destroying the nature of the gospels. This does not yet solve the synoptic problem nor scientifically prove the historical reliability of the gospels. But only from this viewpoint can the origin of the gospels and the role that the early church played in it be approached in an historical manner. If what Mark calls the gospel of Jesus Christ is primarily concerned with the story — or kerygma, if you will — of the historical Jesus, and not with the response of the early church to it, then the early church is in the first place the recipient and not the producer of the tradition. Tradition must have been something sacred and unassailable for the church, with which it could not deal arbitrarily by merely projecting the image of the risen Lord onto the story of Jesus of Nazareth and creating and re-creating words and deeds of Jesus according to its own imagination. There is no proof whatever that tradition in the ancient church was the open arena of religious fantasy. Quite the reverse. All we know about tradition is that its origin and bearers are not an anonymous congregation, but the apostles of the Lord himself. Besides, where could such a church be found, able to produce such a tradition? The image we get from the New Testament of the earliest churches does not allow for the supposition of such genial creativity.

Thus it becomes difficult to accept that the gospels were simply collections of units of tradition spread about in all areas and situations in the church. Tradition must have arisen and formed in a far more consistent unity in the hands of experts and authorized people. Not that there was from the beginning an unassailable formation of the tradition. But a real care for its unity and preservation must have existed in various parts of the church. Luke says in the introduction to his gospel that *many* had undertaken the compilation of a narrative of the things which had been accomplished. And at last the church accepted four different gospels.

All this proves that from the outset there must have been real activity to preserve the tradition. This cannot have been intended in the first place to give historical form and shape to the faith of the community, but on the contrary to recover and preserve as much as possible of the earthly life of Jesus that was important for preaching in and building up the early church.

c. *Not surprisingly, after the form-critical method got lost in endless detail, another approach developed, more directed to the whole of the gospels than to the hypothetical origin of their different parts, the so-called redaction-criticism method.*

The main thesis of this method is that the gospels are the end-product formed by a process of development involving various traditions eventually combined. The gospel writers, however, were not merely compilers and collectors who brought the traditions to some sort of unity for better or for worse. Closer analysis reveals that they arranged things, and from a certain perspective edited and gave form to the traditions to which they had access. Whereas the form-critical method directed its attention to the smaller units of which the tradition was supposed to have originally consisted, the redaction method focuses on the whole gospel, the entire book as the product of the redactional activity of the gospel writers.

This method of approach is in itself nothing new. The well-known commentator Adolf Schlatter (*Der Evangelist Matthäus*, 2nd ed., 1933) showed, for example, that the writer of the first gospel composed his work independently, with a particular goal and a particular speech of his own, and with an eye to the needs of the church in Palestine, in which he found himself and for which he wrote.

The redaction-criticism method continued along these lines:

(1) by tracing, by means of a detailed comparison of Matthew, Mark, and Luke, their typical differences in method of transmission;

(2) by not viewing these differences as proof of arbitrariness or clumsiness, but rather as an indication of the peculiar theological approach of the gospel writers. Thus one speaks of the "theology" of Matthew, of Mark, and of Luke;

(3) by linking these different redactions to the ecclesiastical situation in which the evangelists found themselves. In this respect the redaction-criticism method shows a clear point of contact with the form-critical idea that the tradition should be also interpreted from its *Sitz im Leben*. But the concern here is not only with select parts of the gospels, but with the gospels themselves.

Undoubtedly the danger of kerygmatizing and dehistoriciz-

ing the tradition can arise here too. Because in Matthew
5:17 it is said: "Think not that I have come to abolish the law
and the prophets" and then in the Sermon on the Mount,
which follows, a detailed explication of the law is given, some
advocates of the redaction-criticism method argue that there is
proof here that in the church of Matthew's time the problem
of the law had become acute. They consider that a sort of
antinomianism had arisen over against Judaism and that
Matthew in this passage takes his stand against it.

Now it may indeed be that there was an antinomian tendency in a part of the early church, but then in the explication of this verse the question of historicity inevitably
arises. In the first place, did Jesus really say these words, or
did Matthew put them in his mouth in order rightly to combat
later antinomianism in his name? In other words, does Matthew 5:17 have its *Sitz im Leben* only in the situation of the
later church or also already in the situation of Jesus' life? In
the second place, if Jesus spoke these words, then they were
not directed against antinomianism, but against the objections
óf the Pharisees, who contended that Jesus intended to abolish
the law and the prophets. In other words, when the redac-
tion-critical method interprets the sense of the words on the
basis of the situation of the early church, then their point
becomes something entirely different from what it would be
if they were explained with a view to the situation of the
earthly Jesus.

To be sure, it is quite possible that Jesus' words were later
put into a completely different historical context (this happens when one makes a sermon, too) and that they came quite
easily to have a somewhat different nuance from what they
had had in Jesus' situation. These words of Jesus are then
used for another purpose than they originally were given for.
In my opinion one cannot regard this as impermissible. Still,
it is necessary first of all to ask what the original sense of the
passage was, and the later ecclesiastical interpretation must
not obscure or obliterate the historical meaning, but as much
as possible take its starting point in that historical meaning.

Another example of this redaction-criticism method of interpretation is found in the well-known discussion by Gunther Bornkamm (in Bornkamm, Barth, and Held, *Tradition and Interpretation in Matthew*, 1963, pp. 52-57) of the stilling of the storm (Matt. 8:18-27). Bornkamm first of all calls attention to the fact that this story is preceded in Matthew by the report of three people who wanted to follow Jesus, all of whom were told by Jesus what was involved in following him. The account then continues: "And when he got into the boat, his disciples *followed* him." Then comes the story of the storm and its stilling.

How does Bornkamm interpret this? He combines both passages. After the aphorisms about following Jesus, he says, comes the story of the stilling of the storm as the illustration of what it actually means to follow Jesus in real life. Whoever follows Jesus runs the risk of getting caught in the storm with him. The boat here is the ship of the church. The story is transplanted out of the life of Jesus into the life of the early church. Bornkamm tries then to show how the later redaction of this story is directed more to strengthening the faith of the early church in her trials and tribulations than to the historical miracle of the stilling of the storm. Not that he necessarily regards the miracle as unhistorical — he does not go into that at all — but he interprets the story on the basis of the situation in the early church and its faith in the exalted Lord.

I think Bornkamm gives an excellent interpretation here, since it is not the intention of the gospels to remain at a standstill with the historical Jesus and his miracles on earth. Nevertheless, I think that in the context of Matthew 8 and 9 — the so-called chapters of the miracles in Matthew — the christological viewpoint and not the ecclesiastical dominates. Matthew's intention above anything else is to give a cross-section of the miracles of Jesus in which his omnipotence is revealed with great diversity, including his dominion over the powers of nature. This is the primary and dominant viewpoint. That this is used by the later church in its own situation to instil faith and give consolation does not conflict with that point of view and we should do justice to that viewpoint in our own preaching about this passage. It is equally true that the historical Jesus is also the risen Lord. But the primary intention of the story is to bring clearly into view for us, out of the life of the historical Jesus, the person and the power of the risen Lord. Expressed in another way, the intention of the gospels is not merely to tell us who Jesus *is*, but in the first place who Jesus *was*. This is not a contradiction but a sequence which should dominate our whole view and interpretation of the gospels.

This is not to deny that the redaction-criticism method has been a very fruitful one, especially because it helps us see more clearly the unity of the gospels and the structure and goal of each gospel in particular. It is impossible of course to show this here and now in each of the three gospels separately. I think it is the most difficult with Mark because his is the first gospel, and we do not know his sources. Since they are not available, it is therefore difficult to get to know just how independent he actually was in editing his gospel and what conclusions can be drawn from that. The case is different with Matthew and Luke since they probably were acquainted with and used Mark's gospel. Hence, we can more clearly distinguish their intentions by seeing *how* they used Mark's gospel.

* * *

In order not to deal only in generalities, I would like in closing to look at the gospel of Matthew from this point of view in a little more detail. It has long been observed regarding the structure of this gospel that the sequence of events in its second half (13:53 and after) is more in accord with the gospel of Mark than in the first half. So it is not too farfetched to suppose that the redaction of Matthew comes to the fore more typically in the first half of the gospel than in the second half. This supposition is more probable since the analysis of the first half shows a remarkable architectonic structure in terms of both its proportions and its content. Consider:

(1) With regard to its proportions the gospel as a whole is constructed very harmoniously. Its 1070 verses divide into four nearly equal parts, each consisting in our system of versification of roughly 270 verses.

A. 1:1 — 9:35. Jesus' birth; his appearance in Israel; his ministry in preaching and miracles (270 verses).

B. 9:36 — 16:12. confrontation with Israel (270 verses).

C. 16:13 — 23:39. announcement of his death, the way to the cross (272 verses).

D. 24:1 — 28:20. farewell; suffering, death, and resurrection (258 verses).

(2) The greatest part of Jesus' words is brought together by Matthew into five long discourses of different character, evenly distributed throughout the gospel, each closing with the stereotypical phrase: "And when Jesus had finished these . . ." (7:28; 11:1; 13:53; 19:1; 26:1).

A. Ch. 5-7. sermon on the mount.

B. Ch. 10. sending out the twelve.

C. Ch. 13. parables discourse.

D. Ch. 18. discourse regarding the community of the disciples.

E. Ch. 23-25. discourse against the Pharisees; eschatological discourse.

(3) The most typically "Matthean" part of the gospel covers 1:1 — 13:52 (the 270 verses of A + 180 of B = 450 verses, or 5/12 of the whole). Starting at 13:52 the author follows the sequence of events of Mark (covering 90 verses of B + the 272 of C and the 258 of D = 620 verses, or roughly 7/12 of the totality). This also suggests that the gospel has been built up from units which consist (in our verse-division) of approximately ninety verses (or twice that amount).

(4) A and B, in which (up to 13:52) the evangelist, in addition to his "own" materials (for instance, ch. 1-2), disposes freely of "Marcan" stories (both in sequence and in presentation), display proportionally a very remarkable "chiastic" structure. A falls apart into two sections, of 90 and 180 verses

respectively, and B into two sections of 180 and 90 respectively. In other words the structure of A and B has the pattern of a.b.-b.a. (a=90, b=180 verses).

(5) With reference to their contents also, these various parts of 90, 180, 180, 90 verses show Matthew's architectonic gifts in the formation of his gospel.

A. The first part of A (1:1 − 4:25) clearly forms the introduction to the whole gospel.

Ch. 1-2. genealogy, birth, wise men from the East, flight to Egypt, return to Nazareth;

Ch. 3. John the Baptist; Jesus' baptism;

Ch. 4:1-11. temptation in the wilderness;

Ch. 4:12-25. general characterization of Jesus' ministry: preaching of the gospel (a); miracles (b); company of disciples (c).

total: 90 verses

B. The following 180 verses of A (5:1 − 9:36) correspond with 4:12-25 as far as (a) and (b) are concerned.

Ch. 5-7. illustration of (a): the sermon on the mount;

Ch. 8-9. illustration of (b): the so-called miracles-chapters.

total: 180 verses

C. The first part of B (180 verses, 9:36 − 13:52) presents first of all, in continuation of 5:1 − 9:36, in ch. 10 the third illustration of Jesus' ministry (the instruction of the disciples), corresponding to (c) in 4:12-25. In ch. 11-12 the reaction of all sorts of people to Jesus' ministry, as presented in ch. 5-10, is coming to the fore, showing for the greater part misunderstanding, unbelief, enmity. This leads to the parables in ch. 13, in which Jesus explains the mystery of the kingdom, revealed only to those who have received eyes to see and ears to hear. In summary:

Ch. 10. illustration of (c);

Ch. 11-12. misunderstanding, unbelief, and enmity, beginning with the reaction of John the Baptist;

> Ch. 13. the hiddenness of the kingdom, explained in seven parables.
>
> *total: 180 verses*

From 13:53 the sequence of the events with Mark is followed, starting with Mark 6. The structural grip on the material persists. From now on, however, the cohesion of the different pericopes is more diffuse.

> D. The second part of B (90 verses, 13:53 — 16:12) brings the story to the great caesura of Caesarea Philippi: the announcement of Jesus' suffering and death.
>
> Ch. 13:53 — 16:12. Jesus in continuous confrontation with Israel, up to Caesarea Philippi.
>
> *total: 90 verses*

(6) As to the so-called miracles-chapters (8 and 9), more intensive analysis shows that the miracles narrated here have been very carefully selected by the writer, who includes one of every kind. This is reflected on in 11:5. Chapters 8 and 9 can be further subdivided into four equal parts of 17 verses, in which the miracles of Jesus are seen from a different point of view.

> A. 8:1-17. Jesus takes upon himself the sicknesses of the people in accordance with Isaiah 53;
> B. 8:18-34. Jesus is Lord also of the powers and of demons;
> C. 9:1-17. healing and forgiving go together;
> D. 9:18-34. Jesus is Lord over death. The conclusion (27-34) speaks of the reaction of the people, a motif taken up in chapters 11-12 and extensively elaborated on.

So much for the proportions of the gospel of Matthew. What is revealed is a very purposeful and clearly distinctive redaction. Comparison with the parallel sections in Mark brings the profile of this redaction the more to the fore.

As we could already notice, this structural redaction goes hand in hand with the logical and "theological" points of view from which the architect Matthew is building up his gospel.

After the birth stories (see below), the first goal of Matthew is to give a general image of the greatness of Jesus in his words and deeds, 4:12-25 giving a summary, elaborated successively in chapters 5-7 (preaching), 8-9 (miracles), and 10 (mission of the disciples).

It is Jesus' divine authority in speaking, healing, and disposing of the life of his disciples which here is pointed out in great detail. In chapters 11 and 12 comes the turning-point, so to speak, the negative reaction, both in the misunderstanding of John the Baptist and in the unbelief of the cities of Galilee and the enmity of the leaders of Israel.

The purpose of this picture is unmistakable: revealing and at the same time concealing the messianic glory and kingship of the earthly Jesus. Although Jesus was preaching with absolute authority (unlike the scribes of Israel) and with the same authority healed sick people, ruled over demonic powers, forgave sins, and triumphed over death, even John the Baptist asked, "Are you he who is to come, or shall we look for another?" Even Jesus' predecessor, in spite of the visible fulfillment of Old Testament prophecy in Jesus' powerful words and deeds (11:5), faced the real possibility of taking offense at him (11:6).

This possibility of offense revealed itself in different forms of misunderstanding, neglect, and bitter hostility, aiming at Jesus' death (ch. 11-12). This riddle of unbelief and enmity is to be overcome only by the miracle of the grace of God, who gives the ability to know and to understand the mystery of the kingdom not to the wise and understanding, but to children (11:25ff.). Nevertheless, the kingdom is already revealing itself and nobody can be excused (12:28). But the nature of the kingdom and the way of the King appear different from what people expect and would like to hear and to see. Although the new world is breaking through already, he in whom God reveals his kingdom in mercy and power is misunderstood and rejected by his own people. The structure of the first part of the gospel in particular brings to expression in a wonderful way this ambivalent character of the kingdom, concluding in the chapter of the parables (13), in which Jesus provisionally explains the mystery to his disciples, to whom it has been given to know the secrets of the kingdom of heaven (13:11).

The parable of the sower and the motif of the seed in its relation to the harvest play an important role in this explanation. The kingdom of God is the harvest, bringing the foregoing labor to a wonderful divine result. But for the time being the seed that is sown and the Sower who is sowing depend on all sorts of "natural" influences, even on the most wicked hostility (13:24ff.). The seed, which in the end will be the greatest of shrubs, is the smallest of all seeds. It is in this way that the kingdom is coming, like leaven hidden in the meal, like a treasure hidden in a field, a pearl of great value, which is to be discovered and only to be bought in exchange for all that a person possesses.

This great paradox, the combination of the self-revealing and the self-concealing of the kingdom and of the person of Jesus himself, is the underlying and dominating idea of the marvelous structure and development of the first part of the gospel. And only after having interpreted the tradition in this way and having provided his readers with this understanding, does the author, in the second part of his gospel, join Mark in the course of his story, starting with Mark 6 and bringing all the lines of the history of Jesus together in his sufferings, death, and resurrection.

Undoubtedly it is not only in the structural redaction of the gospel that the "theology" of Matthew is to be sought. It has long been observed that Matthew is the most "Jewish" of the synoptic gospels. Matthew is the evanglist most concerned with the role and the significance of the people of Israel. Evidence for this is found in the genealogy of Jesus Christ in chapter 1, which starts with Abraham, as well as in the many quotations from the Old Testament and in the so-called particularistic sayings in 10:5 and 15:24. On this basis some representatives of the redaction-criticism method locate the *Sitz im Leben* of the first gospel in a typical Jewish-Christian context

and qualify the whole "theology" of Matthew, even in its
soteriological and christological aspects, as Jewish-Christian,
giving Gentiles a share of salvation only insofar as they are
willing to be included in and to adapt themselves to the
Jewish-Christian community as the true people of God.

In present literature, however, a sharp controversy has
risen over this analysis of· the character and purpose of the
gospel, and, in consequence, over its historical *Sitz im Leben*.
Some argue that in order to understand the real meaning of
the gospel one must start with its conclusion, the universal
mission mandate of 28:16-20. All its "Jewishness" would
have no other significance than to serve as background for
the confrontation with the unbelieving Jews, bidding them
farewell and proclaiming the Gentiles as the real heirs of the
kingdom and the new Israel. So the *Sitz im Leben* of the first
gospel would have to be sought in a Gentile-Christian situation, and a more detailed investigation would only confirm
such a conclusion.

Does such an alternative get us on the right track? Is the
redaction of Matthew in fact dominated especially by the
situation in which the evangelist lived and worked and which
he tried to influence? Here, again, the structural redaction
of the gospel can help us. It would seem to point in another
direction, aiming not in the first place at a special situation in
the later church, be it Jewish- or Gentile-Christian, but at a
more general goal.

There is no doubt that, especially in his introductory chapters, the evangelist uses his redactional talents admirably to
make it clear that Jesus is the true representative of Israel. He
arranges Jesus' genealogy so that Jesus is the last in three
groups of fourteen generations, the forty-second of the whole
offspring of Abraham, the one in whom — by the grace of
God and the power of the Holy Spirit — the people of Israel
has reached its destination and fulfilment. Chapter 2 continues this line of thinking. Jesus represents Israel again when
already as a child he, like Moses, was made the object of the
wrath and oppression of foreign tyrants, fulfilling in this soli-

darity the loud lamentations of Rachel, the mother of Israel. Like Israel, however, he was saved by God's wonderful intervention, and was called from Egypt as the son of God. In the redaction of Matthew 4, Jesus' temptation in the wilderness fits neatly into this pattern, as do his answers to the tempter from Deuteronomy, recalling Israel's temptations in the wilderness and its failure to answer in the right way. All this shows clearly enough, already in the first few chapters, that only in his identification with Israel can Jesus be seen in the right light.

But at the same time, the Gentiles are involved from the very beginning in the redaction of Matthew. In the genealogy they are represented by the non-Jewish women, who are mentioned purposely and significantly as the mothers of Israel, sometimes at the very turning-points of its history. In chapter 2 it is the wise men of the East who come into view as soon as Jesus is born. Certainly they had to be taught by the scribes of Israel in order to find their way to Bethlehem, but they were the only ones who recognized and worshiped in the child of Joseph and Mary the King of the Jews. And, to mention one more example from Matthew's structural redaction, when he arranges Jesus' miracles in chapters 8 and 9, the first healing is that of the leprous *Jew*, laying stress on the full observation of the Jewish law for the lepers; but the next one is the curing of the servant of the *Gentile* centurion, purposely placed in this context in addition to the miracles of Mark and apart from the context in which Luke tells this story. The faith of this centurion is called greater than any Jesus found in Israel, this centurion being the forerunner of the many who will came from east and west and sit at table with Abraham, Isaac, and Jacob, while the sons of the kingdom will be thrown out. This does not mean the rejection of Israel, for the centurion is just one of the many in Israel who are blessed and whose faith is praised too.

In this arrangement we notice a line of thought observable through the whole gospel. It is always the Christ of Israel who is the center, only to be understood in the light of Israel's prophecy, the fulfiller of the powerful deeds of God's salvation in the past. But it is this Christ who is also the Savior of the Gentiles, not incorporating them in Israel in a particularistic way but extending the grace of Israel's God to all peoples of the world in the most universal sense of the word. Focusing our attention on the whole of the gospel (as the redaction method does), we are allowed to conclude that there is far more intrinsic unity and cohesion in the tradition itself than the atomic approach of the form-critical method suggests. Otherwise it would not have been possible for Matthew (for example) to give us such a coherent and impressive image of the person and the story of Jesus of Nazareth. This means at the same time that this picture is not in the first place the result of reflection and interpretation only in behalf of the cares and problems of a specific local or regional church, but, on the contrary, an attempt to bring these specific and different aspects of the church's *Sitz im Leben* into the wide horizon of the redemptive history of Jesus' life, death, and resurrection, as these have been the very core and heart of the existing tradition.

At least as far as the gospel of Matthew is concerned, we can now say that this christological point of view very clearly dominates the ecclesiastical and not the reverse. It is also for that reason that these gospels have been received by the churches in all places and times as the story and the kerygma of Jesus of Nazareth, the Messiah of Israel, the Savior of the world.

4.

The Christology of
the Fourth Gospel:
History and Interpretation

THE WAY THE IMAGE of Jesus is depicted in the fourth gospel continues to arouse discussion. There is often talk of the "riddle" of the fourth gospel — the totally unique witness of this book to the person and the work of Jesus Christ in his life on earth, a witness that seems quite removed from the historical Jesus-image of the synoptics. In other words, it is the relation between the historical reality of Jesus' life and John's interpretation of this reality — which can be called (for better or worse) his Christology — which is continually under consideration in biblical and dogmatic theology. Some recent developments in this discussion bring to the fore what in my opinion is essential for understanding the fourth gospel and solving its so-called riddle.

Some scholars feel that the fourth gospel bears the character of a theological interpretation to such an extent that they deny the author any historical intention at all. This does not mean that he could not have been a good historian, but rather that he has consciously and purposely portrayed the image of Jesus in a mystical or symbolic way. His purpose was not to recount history, but to express his ideas about the divine person and message of Jesus in historical images. Although these idealistic and mystical interpretations of the gospel (for instance, that of F. C. Baur, father of the Tübingen school, and that of A. Loisy, the French priest noted for his part in the so-called "modernist controversy") do not receive much support nowadays, radical historical criticism of the fourth gospel is still alive. For Bultmann, in his well-known commentary, the gospel has hardly any historical value. What counts for him is John's *interpretation*. The characteristic of this book, according to Bultmann, is that the works of Jesus as the Revelator are described in the language of mythology, specifically in what he calls the gnostic myth of the Redeemer, a supernatural being who descends from heaven, brings people real knowledge, and then returns to God. On the gnostic conception of reality, however, the glory *(doxa)* of the Redeemer is a hidden glory, visible only to those who are able to discern this glory with the eyes of faith, to people who are spiritually sighted, not blind. According to this underlying gnostic conception the key-word in the gospel, "The word became flesh" (John 1:14), is to be understood in terms of the complete hiddenness of the revelation, which is designated by the word "flesh." This saying means: the word became man and nothing else but a man. This is the great paradox, the *skandalon* in the revelation of Jesus Christ. He came to reveal the glory of God, but there was in him nothing glorious or divine that could be seen and recognized other than by faith. The Christology of the fourth gospel as Bultmann explains it therefore appears to be of a *kenotic* nature.

To be sure, Bultmann is aware that the fourth gospel also contains a number of tremendous miracles, in which the glory of the Redeemer seems to reveal itself in all clarity for the eyes of all persons. But Bultmann does not consider that the miracles in the fourth gospel had this significance for the author. In relating the miracles in their spectacular form, he was merely joining the tradition. For him miracles had only symbolic significance; they meant nothing in themselves. They are just another sort of kerygma and can mean something only for those who understand their deeper, symbolic reality. The whole gospel is therefore nothing but a mythological expression of the kerygma that in the encounter with Jesus Christ one is confronted with the word of God. Not the knowledge of the "historical Jesus," but the existentialistic decision (*Entscheidung*) with which he confronts us, is important.

Remarkable is the criticism of Bultmann by the well-known

scholar Ernst Käsemann. On the one hand, as a pupil of Bultmann, coming out of the same radical tradition, he approaches the historical reliability of the gospel no less critically than does Bultmann. According to Käsemann, the fourth gospel, measured by our concept of reality, is more fantastic than any other book of the New Testament. He, too, believes that the book originated in heretical circles of a gnostic character and that the evangelist has described the historical Jesus on the basis of a gnostic concept of reality. That is why he could work with the historical tradition so freely and imaginatively, because historicity in itself does not have much value for the gnostic. On the other hand, Käsemann's conception of the Christology of the fourth gospel is precisely the opposite of Bultmann's interpretation. While Bultmann argues that the glory of Jesus in the fourth gospel is a totally hidden one and the Redeemer became man and no more than man, Käsemann says that the fourth gospel is surely meant to give a description of the abundant glory of Jesus in the flesh. His is a completely different — and, in my opinion, much better — explanation of John 1:14. Of course it reads "the Word became *flesh*," but then follows "and dwelt among us . . . and we have beheld his glory." The incarnation was not a means of *concealing* the glory, but in fact of *revealing* it. It is the glory of the divine Logos of God, which has revealed itself in overwhelming majesty in the flesh, which has empowered him to perform the greatest miracles, which enabled him to dispute with his opponents with unlimited superiority, which resulted in his going into death as the triumphant one. That is why one cannot by means of demythologizing the gospel remove the divinity of Jesus without destroying the core of the gospel. The image of Christ in John is not that of a man and nothing but a man, but rather of God walking on the earth. And according to Käsemann, this is how it is intended. The gospel is not simply concerned with the kerygma, in the existentialistic sense of that word, but especially with the *person* of Jesus. The witness of the divinity of Jesus is really the content of the message of John — in sharp antithesis to what Bultmann says.

Käsemann's explanation of the intention of the fourth gospel strikes me as far nearer the truth than Bultmann's. With Bultmann all things center on the existentialistic message of the decision the individual has to take *against* the visible world, *against* what is available for us and what we can dominate ourselves, and *in favor of* the invisible world, which is not within our reach. This is the only way a person can really become human. And it is, in Bultmann's view, the "christological" message of the fourth gospel that it brings us to this confrontation, to this paradoxical decision, as the only way of freedom and salvation. The big issue in the fourth gospel is therefore not Christology as such but anthropology; not the nature of Christ but the nature of salvation.

It is exactly in this respect that Käsemann differs from Bultmann. The dogma of the fourth gospel is not that of Bultmann's demythologizing and existentialistic interpretation, but is the dogma of the revelation of Jesus Christ in his divine glory as the Son of God. This christological dogma in the real sense of the word is the very core and heart of the message that confronts us in the fourth gospel. That is why, Käsemann says, the church has accepted this gospel in spite of its possibly heretical origins and that is why the church even today cannot evade a confrontation with this message without thereby setting aside the real meaning and purpose of the gospel of John.

In this respect Käsemann's criticism is on target. Soteriology depends on Christology, and you cannot change this order. But the consequence of this position, it seems to me, is that the question of historicity comes back with its full force. According to Käsemann the Christology of the fourth gospel has a naive, docetic character, originating in its gnostic background, revealing itself in its free and sometimes fantastic treatment of the historical tradition. But how then can we possibly accept the real message of this gospel, as Käsemann has pointed it out so consistently, without falling back into a new (or old!) idealistic Christology, in which at decisive moments a spiritualistic ideology has to replace the failing historical revelation? This is the Achilles' heel of Käsemann's attempt to combine an unbiased interpretation of John's message with radical historical criticism.

More and more students of the fourth gospel are becoming convinced that an ahistorical approach to it is untenable, whether in the idealistic manner of F. C. Baur or the existentialistic manner of Rudolf Bultmann. It cannot be denied that John wanted to write history. The gospel as a whole, with all its historical, chronological, and topographical details, is proof of this. Therefore one can observe a turn in the tide of opinion, in the judgment also of many whom one cannot reproach with undue conservatism or fundamentalism. C. H. Dodd, for instance, argues that the gospel of John undoubtedly is more a theological than a historical work, but he strongly maintains its historical basis and value.

There are recent indications which point emphatically to Palestine for the historical background of the gospel and, indeed, to a time before the fall of Jerusalem. The accuracy of various topographical references in the gospel has been established by such experts in Palestinian archaeology as W. F. Albright and Joachim Jeremias. Since the excavation of Bethesda and its colonnades it can no longer be maintained that the five arcades mentioned in John 5 were only symbols of the five books of Moses, as some people used to do. It is no less important that the Qumran writings have opened up a rich source of comparable material proving at least that for the explanation of various Johannine ideas and motives it is not necessary to look so far afield as has often been supposed.

One cannot maintain that to the evangelist of the fourth gospel only the kerygma and not history is important. What he — like the other gospel writers but in his own way — tried to make clear was that Jesus' life was filled with the glory of God. He recorded everything so that his readers would believe that *this* Jesus of history, who dwelt among us, is the Christ, the Son of God (20:31). The story of this Jesus must bring forth faith; faith has not brought forth the story, much less the history. This is no less fundamental for understanding the fourth gospel than for the other three.

Nevertheless, there is interpretation of history, too, in all four gospels. But in the gospel of John the element of interpretation is extremely important and, I think, manifest. This is perhaps why the historical meaning and character of the gospel have been doubted, misunderstood, and rejected again and again.

* * *

This element of the interpretation of history is dominant in the gospel from its very beginning. Everything told about Jesus stands in the supra-earthly glory of the prologue, the glory of the Logos who was with God, in whom was God. This is the glory *(doxa)* which dominates the whole gospel. In John this glory is not only the projection of the later glory of the resurrection of Christ, but is the glory of the pre-existent Son of God, the glory from the beginning. It is perfectly clear that the evangelist, by placing the whole story of Jesus in the light of this prologue, intends to give a very special interpretation to the story of Jesus of Nazareth.

Other evangelists give their interpretations of this history, too. But there are real differences between John and the synoptics. The gospel of Matthew, for instance, also has an all-dominating prologue — the genealogy of Jesus of Nazareth, which is traced back to Abraham. But it makes a difference whether the interpretation of the history of Jesus has its starting point in Abraham or in the eternal Logos who was in the beginning. The question may arise whether the glory is not overexposed in John. Can the abundant glory in which John places the history of Jesus be harmonized with the humanity of Jesus and not conflict with the reservation which was typical in Jesus' self-revelation — not only in the synoptics, but also in John's gospel itself? In his farewell discourse (recorded in John 14-17), Jesus himself says: "I have yet many things to say to you, but you cannot bear them now. When the Spirit of truth comes, he will guide you into all truth. . . . He will glorify me, for he will take what is mine and declare it to you" (John 16:12ff.). And yet, time and again in the gospel it is as if the veil has been removed already and Jesus speaks without this reservation, for example, when he says of himself "before Abraham was, I am" (8:58), or when he speaks of the glory he had with the Father before the world was (17:5,24), or when he says that the disciples will see the Son of Man ascend to "where he was before" (6:62).

There are indications that in his description John is already removing the veil lying over the revelation of the earthly Jesus. Indeed, we sometimes do not know for sure who has the word in this gospel, the earthly Jesus or the gospel writer who witnesses about him. This is especially true of those curious parts in John 3 — verses 12-21 and 31-46 — where, as in the prologue, Jesus is spoken of in the third person: not "whoever believes in *me*," but "whoever believes in *him*." But also in passages where Jesus is introduced in the first person, he sometimes speaks in an undisguised fashion about his pre-existent glory, and then it seems as if all boundaries between his eternal and earthly existence disappear.

At this point we have to take into consideration again what Jesus said to his disciples in the last discourses about their future witness to him. Among other things, he said that when he himself was no longer with them, the Holy Spirit would teach them everything and remind them of all he had said to them (14:26). Exactly the same thing is said in 15:26: "*he* will be a witness to me; and *you* also are witnesses, because *you* have been with me from the beginning." There is thus a close connection between those who were with Jesus from the beginning as ear- and eye-witnesses and the witness of the Spirit. The operation of the Spirit will be more than merely sharpening the memory of the apostles concerning the exact words of Jesus; it will also be teaching them, expounding all that Jesus had taught.

It may rightly be asked whether we are here given an indication, a clear hint, that the evangelist is himself aware that he is giving the words of Jesus in a new interpretative and creative form. This might explain the words of 16:25 that

Jesus has up to now spoken in figures (*paroimiais*), but that the hour is coming when he will speak plainly of the Father. May we assume that that hour comes in the gospel itself when (in our judgment) the veil is already removed and Jesus seems to speak freely of his Father? In other words, here in the testimony of the evangelist to the readers of the gospel the Spirit, who explicates everything, is already jointly having the word. Through the Spirit as his witness Jesus is speaking plainly of the Father, also in the words of the gospel. That is why there is this sort of duality: on the one hand the tradition and the memory of John as eyewitness, on the other the teaching by the Spirit, as a result of which there comes about the removal of the veil which had been laid over the self-revelation of the glory of Jesus.

Perhaps we can say that the historical image gets, as a result, a surplus value, because it is seen now in the light not only of the later exaltation of Jesus, but before all things in the light of the Logos, who was from the beginning. This image of the historical Jesus is not only drawn with the help of memory and tradition, but also with the aid of the Spirit. The Spirit taught them who Jesus really was and what was the secret of his glory. And John himself refers for this image to what Jesus had promised him and the other apostles in his last discourses with them.

*   *   *

As a result of this does the image of Jesus given by John become less historical, even docetic? Is the fourth gospel (as some have said) the gospel of a God wandering over the earth, no longer the gospel of the man Jesus of Nazareth? I think it can scarcely be questioned that John himself regards Jesus as a real man. You can even quote the fourth gospel especially to prove that Jesus was a man of flesh and blood. It is the gospel of John which lays stress on the fact that water and blood came out of the side of the dead Jesus; that, in his life, he showed human needs, became tired and thirsty, wept at the grave of his friend, was deeply moved by the prospect of his

own impending death (19:34; 6:7; 11:35; 12:27). In addition
the gospel constantly mentions Jesus' *obedience* to the will of
his Father, to which he had to *submit* himself, even when this
would lead him into deep *humiliation*. All this can scarcely be
contested.

But the question remains whether it is not true that all
these human traits and features are deeply overshadowed by
Jesus' divine glory and his unity with his Father, so that his
humanity is totally absorbed by his deity and his incarnation
(1:14) is nothing but a temporary medium through which
God's glory in him was revealed to the people. According to
Käsemann, who styles the Christology of the fourth gospel as
naïve and docetic, this docetism is especially evident in the
way John speaks about the death of Jesus. In the fourth gospel,
according to Käsemann, the glory of Jesus so controls the total
development that fitting in the passion becomes a problem. It
comes into the picture only at the end, as a sort of appendix.
Naturally the gospel-writer could not bypass Jesus' death. He
finally solves the problem by describing the passion as a sort of
glorification. The cross is no longer the accursed tree but the
proof of his divine love and his glorified return out of the exile
to the Father. That is why, with a peculiar word-play, the
fourth gospel sometimes speaks about the cross as the exaltation
of Jesus (3:14; 8:28; 12:32, 34) and other times as his glorification (7:39; 12:16,23; 13:31; 17:1,5).

Still, with this not everything has been said about John's
interpretation of Jesus' death. Even though on his way to
the cross Jesus showed himself to be the mightiest (the officers
and soldiers arresting him in Gethsemane fell down; 18:6), John
describes his suffering from other viewpoints as well — for
instance, from the viewpoint of humiliation and self-surrender
as the bitter cup his Father gives him to drink (18:11); and
as "hating of his life" (12:25). Also it becomes abundantly
clear that John sees the death and self-humiliation of Jesus
as necessary for those who belong to him. Only when the
grain of wheat falls into the earth and dies does it bear fruit
(12:24). Jesus is, according to the word of the high priest, the

one who dies *for* the people (11:50,51). For their sake he sanc-
tifies himself; that means he consecrates himself to death
(17:19) and only if he washes their feet in humiliation do they
have a part with him. Thus John the Baptist, at the very beginning of this gospel, can call Jesus the Lamb of God who took
away the sins of the world. In all this we have not even spoken
of the so-called sacramental discourses (John 6), in which Jesus
speaks of the eating of his flesh and the drinking of his blood
as the meat and drink for eternal life. No matter how much in
the fourth gospel's description of the death of Jesus his glorification receives strong emphasis, it is not yet the case that his
death is nothing but a return, a passage, an exaltation. The
writer of the fourth gospel not only presupposes the Christian
tradition with regard to the meaning of Jesus' death (cf. also 1
John 2:2), but he also brings it to expression, though partially
and incidentally. This also means that the flesh was not only
the medium of the revelation of his glory, but also the way
he had to sacrifice himself for his people (10:11), bearing
their sins.

All these features can hardly be reconciled with a docetic
Christology. Quite properly others have pointed out that it
would be more correct — on their grounds — to call the
Christology of the fourth gospel anti-docetic. They also appeal
for this opinion to the first letter of John, which clearly and
purposely rejects docetism: "Every spirit which confesses that
Jesus Christ has come in the flesh is of God, and every spirit
which does not confess Jesus is not of God. This is the spirit
of antichrist" (1 John 4:2,3).

Still, the more firmly this is maintained, the more the question comes to the fore of how it all can be harmonized with
the mighty, actually blinding light that floods through the
whole of the fourth gospel from the prologue in chapter 1.
Can one really speak of incarnation and of being man when
the subject of the incarnation is the Logos, who has been with
God and has been God before the world was? The question
comes up anew when Jesus testifies of himself "before Abraham was, I am" and when he prays in chapter 17 that God will

glorify him with the glory he had with God before the world was. Is the humanity not inevitably absorbed in the divinity, the *vere homo* sacrificed to the *vere deus?* Is such a Christology "from above" not automatically docetic, and can there be a starting point for a genuinely non-docetic Christology other than the revelation of the historical Jesus — which means a Christology "from below"?

I am not here asking how we can fathom the mystery of the incarnation of the Son of God. Nor is it my intention to go into the dogmatic formulations the church has used in its efforts to bring to expression the mystery in human words (pre-eminently at Chalcedon, but also afterwards). All those questions and definitions are coming up again in the present theological discussion, especially the formula of the un-personal human nature of Christ. I am not suggesting that I can answer all these questions. All I mean to discuss here is the question of exegesis and biblical theology: How could the author of the fourth gospel, who spoke (as we have seen) so massively about the humanity of Christ (even after his resurrection; cf. 20:20,27; 21:13) and did not shrink from the tremendous harshness of the expression that the Logos "became flesh," at the same time make in his prologue the divine Logos the subject of his whole gospel? This question is related to another old problem: How did our author come to know and understand the Logos itself?

*   *   *

To start with the last question, there is a tendency to think that the gospel-writer had previously had a certain dogmatic or philosophical knowledge of the figure of the Logos and that in the light of that knowledge he wanted to acquaint his readers with the person of Jesus. This is the presupposition of all interpretations which say that John derived the figure of the Logos from the religious philosophy of that time — from Philo or the Hermetic writings (as C.H. Dodd suggests) or from gnosis (Bultmann's view) — to introduce Jesus in this way to his hellenistic contemporaries. This is indeed a Christology "from above," from a transcendent a priori — in this case the philosophical abstraction of a Logos, no matter from whatever syncretistic origin it comes.

It seems to me that there are insurmountable objections to this interpretation. First of all, the idea of such an abstract, philosophical, more or less personified Logos, who would have stood as a kind of intermediate principle or being between God and man is apparently not the motive for the author of the fourth gospel to start his prologue with the opening words of the Torah. Furthermore, in the following chapters of the gospel any hint that the name Logos would point to such a philosophical background is lacking. There is in other words nothing in the fourth gospel even to favor such an interpretation of the name Logos, much less to warrant speaking in terms of proof for it.

The question is thus justified the more: How can anyone imagine that the evangelist would have taken as the all-dominating starting point of his message such a philosophical abstraction? His whole gospel, as a matter of fact, consists of a witness to the total uniqueness of Christ. How could he then have reduced this witness to the lowest common denominator and made it dependent on a figure out of the syncretistic religiosity or philosophy of his time?

The real key to understanding John's speaking of the Logos must be sought in the identity of the opening of the prologue and that of Genesis 1:1 — "in the beginning." This is confirmed by the opening of the first epistle of John: the Logos of which the evangelist is speaking is the dynamic, creating word of God which called the world into being. To be sure Genesis 1 does not speak of the Logos in the personal sense of John 1. Some have explained this "personalization" with reference to parallels in the wisdom-literature, where Wisdom is also introduced as speaking from the beginning. Likewise the Torah is sometimes described as being from the beginning with God. By analogy, John is said to have spoken of the Logos as the personified word of God. But still the difference is essential. The Logos in the prologue of John is not just a personification but a Person, and, at the same time, a person of whom it is said that he was with God and that he was God — an idea that has no analogy whatever within the framework of traditional Jewish thinking but would have been judged there as totally unacceptable if not blasphemous.

Therefore, John's concept of the Logos cannot be classified with contemporary pagan and Jewish speculations or person-ifications, without thereby infringing on its unique character. What must come to the fore here is not John's indebtedness to contemporary religious or philosophical ideas about creation, but the overwhelming revelation of the historical Jesus him-self. When the evangelist wants to express the glory of him whose witness he is, he cannot speak of this glory in any other way but in divine categories, because this glory exceeds everything that preceded him in history, even the glory of Moses. That is why the evangelist falls back on the dynamic creating word in the beginning of all God's ways, the word that called forth light out of darkness and created life: the Logos of life that was from the beginning. "The life was made manifest and we saw it, and testify to it, and proclaim to you the eternal life which was with the Father and was made manifest to us" (1 John 1:2).

What is new is that in the prologue to the gospel and in the opening of John's first letter this word and light and life are introduced as a person, albeit that the person and his salva-tory significance are spoken of alternately. We might better say that Logos has not yet become the standard title of the pre-existent Son of God. What is said of the Logos can be said of the Light, too: that it has been with the Father from the beginning. It is not just the name of the Logos that counts, it is he himself, who was in the beginning, who also can be named Life and Light, who has been revealed now. For what is said is that God's creative speaking from the beginning, his light- and life-bringing word, has become flesh and blood in Jesus Christ and has dwelt among us. And so from now on this word, this life, this light can be spoken of in the personal categories of *"he was"* and *"I am."* What brought the evangelist from the divine deeds to the person is not the philosophical material from another religious world, but the beholding of God's glory in Christ about which he speaks in John 1:14.

The reflection on this and the giving of the name in the concrete sense of John 1:1 were certainly matters of time, or better, matters of the witness of those who have been with Jesus from the beginning. We may point out here that in the Old Testament and later Judaism when expression had to be given to the divine character, whether of the Messiah or the law or wisdom, it was often referred back to the glory of God in the beginning. One could say that lines had been drawn into which reflection could move itself. But what a prophet or a pious Jew was never able to say John said, because the proper explanation of this speaking about Christ as the Logos lies in the way the glory of God revealed itself in the person of Jesus. "He who was from the beginning" is not just a personification or idealization of how the divine glory *functioned* in the life of Jesus of Nazareth, as the wisdom and the law can be glorified in pre-existent personifications. It was the oneness of his person and his work, of what he did and who he was, it was the revealing of his unity with the Father, not only in love and obedience but also in will and authority, which empowered the evangelist to speak about Jesus Christ as he did in the prologue.

Therefore, the point of departure of the prologue does not lie genetically in the eternal Logos but in the historical Jesus. John does not speak about Jesus on the basis of a certain pre-knowledge of the Logos; he can speak as he does about the Logos only because he had come to know Jesus. That is why it is not strange that the name of the Logos is not mentioned any further in the gospel. Jesus Christ is the great subject of the gospel and on the basis of his revelation, it is possible to speak of the Logos as is done in 1:1-4. This does not mean that the Logos has become an attribute of or a fancy name for the early Jesus. No, in order to know who Jesus is one has to go back to the beginning. Without knowing how wide and high and deep the work of God has been at the beginning, one cannot understand the dimensions of the glory, of the grace, and of the truth of Jesus Christ. But the converse is also true: to be able to speak in this way, one must have seen the glory of Jesus Christ. Nobody has ever seen God, and nobody will ever know him as he is, unless that person has seen the glory of him who dwelt among us. And that is the story of Jesus of Nazareth. John is a gospel-writer, not "after all" but from the very beginning of his book. Like his predecessor, he testifies and witnesses about Jesus as he *was* when he walked and dwelt among us.

If we may understand the "Christology" of the fourth gospel in this way (and that is, even in its most profound and divine pronouncements, an approach "from below"), then the humanity of Jesus cannot be regarded as docetic. Without the revelation in the flesh — that is, without his entry into history and into the depth of human existence — the glory of the Son of God would not have been revealed. Without this humanity there could not possibly have been talk of the divine person in this distinctiveness. This does not solve all the problems concerning the person of Jesus Christ. In the gospel of John the human character of his feelings, his deliberations, his decisions cannot be doubted for a moment (cf., for example, 12:27ff.; 19:26). At the same time there is, especially in the "I am" sayings, a consciousness of power, authority, and oneness with God, which appears to transcend the human ego. Thus we should avoid on the one hand a onesidedness which, fully recognizing the divine image of Jesus in the fourth gospel, does not find sufficient place for its humanness and ends up in a docetic Christology; and on the other hand the conception that the true human nature and ego of Jesus Christ can only be maintained if the pre-existence of Christ as the Son of God, the Logos who was with God and who was God, is understood as a theological postulate, an ideal glorification of God's revelation in the man of Nazareth. For the way the glory of God in the fourth gospel reveals itself personally in the flesh and blood of Jesus Christ supposes a pre-existence by nature, not just in idea alone.

It is another question whether we can do more than avoid onesidedness in either direction, whether we can subsume under one formula what the author of the fourth gospel testified about the glory of God in the flesh of Jesus. My aim in this essay has been no more than to understand this Christology, not on the basis of an abstract conception of the Logos nor a theological presupposition about the nature of the Son of God, but on the basis of the historical revelation of God in Christ.

5.

The Biblical Message
of Reconciliation

THERE IS TODAY a renewed interest in the biblical concepts of "reconciliation," "liberation," and "renewal." In many instances this interest carries with it an interpretation of these terms that differs from the traditional one. Whereas numerous churches and religious movements have long understood reconciliation in a strictly personal and religious sense, the focus of attention today is increasingly on the significance of reconciliation of social relationships — in particular political and racial ones. Traditionally self-oriented, church and theology have shifted their attention to the outside. Theology is no longer dominated by the personalist and existentialist points of view found in such thinkers as Bultmann. Instead, the questions raised by modern critiques of society are the ones to which theologians are trying to find answers on the basis of and in the light of the gospel. These questions must determine the relevance of the biblical message for our times.

It is not easy to pinpoint a single cause for this remarkable and rather sudden shift of concentration to the social and political implications of the biblical message of reconciliation. One may point out that the immense problems of human society in both the international and national contexts impinge on us more than ever before because of the vast amount of direct information reaching us by way of the press, radio, and television. No less important are the hard-hitting critiques of society which young intellectuals in North America and Western Europe have raised during the last decade under the influence of neo-Marxism and Leninism. Many persons in the churches accept this dynamic and often revolutionary movement as a challenge which merits a biblical response that is adequate socially and politically. In addition we may point to the vast problems with which the underdeveloped nations confront us during this postcolonial era, problems which should plague the conscience of affluent nations. Moreover, the Christian churches in those liberated (and not yet liberated) countries do not cease to demand of international church bodies that they translate the gospel of reconciliation into terms of peace and justice and take the lead in waging war against all forms of racial and economic discrimination. Only so, it is argued, can the gospel become understandable to the world's non-white population. That explains the appearance, for instance, of "black theology."

Not only have these developments occasioned major changes and shifts in church and theology, but they have also led to serious conflicts and oppositions. The essence of human nature is no longer sought first of all in personal self-realization but in the way the human being is involved in history and in the structures of society. Though one must be careful with the distinction between horizontal and vertical, we may say that the horizontal implications of the gospel are receiving heavy emphasis while the vertical ones tend to be overlooked. The vertical relationship to God is still presupposed, but it determines the direction of attention to a lesser degree than does the horizontal relation to other people. Repeatedly we hear that our relationship to God and love for him must prove themselves in relation to our love for our neighbor — in the most universal sense of that word. This is sometimes put in terms of a distinction between micro- and macro-ethics; and it is the latter that is getting all the emphasis lately.

A second major feature of this shift, closely related to the first, is the strong concentration on this earthly and temporal life. The hereafter is a blank entry on the theological balance-sheet. Christians should indeed strive for a different world, but they must not look for it above or after this one, for they should seek it *in* this world. The answer to the question "Are you saved?" must not refer primarily to heaven but to this earth. Expectations for the future do play an important part in this concept of Christianity. This is considered to be of a piece with the messianic longing that appears in the Old Testament and with the future character of the kingdom of God in the New. But we must not look for the fulfilment of this hope in heaven. The Scriptures do speak of a future apocalyptic breakthrough of God's kingdom. To the extent that this newer theology deals with this message, however, it considers it to be only a completion of what confronts human responsibility now.

In this context, concepts of continuity and discontinuity tend to crop up. To the extent that God's great future is not simply the outcome of the renewal of human life now taking place, we are to speak of discontinuity. But complete discontinuity is not considered possible. What can be expected is the harvest of what is accomplished now, during the present dispensation; and that implies continuity, growth, of a future being worked out now. The advent of Christ and of the expected kingdom, then, cover the gap rather than highlight the chasm separating this world from the coming kingdom of God. "Behold, I make all things new" — the theme of the 1968 World Council of Churches assembly in Uppsala — is a promise of God's future only if it can first function as a program for human action in the present.

A third feature is a waning interest in the church as institution in favor of a growing interest in world affairs. Not only is the church's calling to be situated in this world enough to warn it against all forms of egocentricity and self-inversion, but the church's future must be wholly linked with that of the world. For God's reconciliation and Christ's kingship are not limited to the church, but embrace much more. The church may have knowledge of them; it is, as it were, confidentially let in on God's secret; it knows what the world does not as yet know. But it is not knowing alone that counts, but above all doing. Indeed, some go so far as to say that where reconciliation and renewal are being done, there we find the kingdom of Christ, whether people are aware of it or not. Christ's kingship is not church-bound, it is present wherever the forces of renewal and deliverance operate in the reconciliation taking place among persons, nations, and races.

The implications of this new theory of reconciliation are far-reaching. It would be unfair to evaluate it solely with reference to its most radical exponents. In any event this movement does not want to be understood as a secularization of the biblical message. Where it speaks of "radicalization" it is to take seriously what *the Bible* calls reconciliation here and now. The starting point for this entire train of thought is the Christian's basic confession of Christ's lordship, even though this lordship is said to concern not just, or not even primarily, the church but the world in the most universal sense of the term. As for reconciliation, from the vantage-point which Christ offers there can no longer be any room for discrimination among people by reason of lineage, sex, culture, or color of skin, for all of these barriers have been abolished in Christ. The focus is on the effect of the gospel's message of reconciliation: on relationships among people. Is this not precisely the effect God intended with the message and ministry of reconciliation? Did he not love us in order that we should love our neighbor? And could there be a love of God which is not expressed in love of fellow man? Does our love of God not in fact consist in the love of the oppressed and afflicted? Does not Jesus himself teach us that "as you did it to one of the least of these my brethren, you did it to me?" Hence must we not say that the one who loves his brother loves God as well?

This effect of reconciliation constitutes the basis for a renewed interpretation of the entire biblical message. Many central biblical notions and concepts, such as kingdom of God, resurrection, messianic expectation, and conversion have been reinterpreted in the light of this concept of the message of reconciliation. If the biblical message is not to be left on the sidelines as an imperviously mysterious doctrine about transcendent truths relevant only within the hallowed confines of the church, if it is to be relevant for people today and to acquire some live meaning for them, this message will have to be practiced as a message of renewal and reconciliation.

This new development has encountered powerful opposition within the churches. We may in fact speak of a tendency towards polarization over this issue. The question has to do with a proper understanding of the gospel of reconciliation. Many feel that to the extent that we stress the social implications of the biblical witness we run the risk of bypassing and neglecting the most fundamental human needs, thereby robbing the biblical concept of reconciliation of its power. Is our personal relationship to God not the central concern of the biblical message of reconciliation? And does not the ministry of reconciliation, to the extent that it affects our neighbor, consist first of all in proclaiming the good news of God's love to that neighbor and living in spiritual communion with him, rather than in trying to accomplish a ministry of reconciliation in the areas of social and political structures?

Many Christians will readily suffer considerable hardship in missionary activity among the nations and races of the world while showing scant concern for racial segregation, colonization, and *apartheid*. These are dismissed as "worldly structures," in which a person lives but which are not essential for salvation. It is of much greater consequence that a human being acquire citizenship in heaven, that his soul be saved, that his future in eternity be secured. Small wonder that those who think this way are suspicious of church leaders who demonstrate for human rights and against colonialism and *apartheid*. They oppose the World Council of Churches for providing humanitarian aid to movements that are engaged in armed struggle to procure liberty, such as the Program to Combat Racism. Such a program, it is thought, turns the biblical message of reconciliation into its opposite: instead of teaching men to expect salvation from God, the church enters the scene as counsel and defense for those who take the law into their own hands. How could that possibly tie in with the biblical message of reconciliation through the blood and spirit of Christ? Does it not secularize the church and the word it preaches to such an extent that we may no longer consider this seriously to be an interpretation of the biblical message?

In the midst of such great spiritual confusion, there is good reason to reflect anew on the actual material content of the biblical message of reconciliation. I take my point of departure in what follows at the heart of the gospel in the New Testament. I do not wish to imply that the Old Testament does not contain this message or that its proclamation of the law constitutes a bleak backdrop to the New Testament message of grace and reconciliation. Quite the contrary. What reconciliation is, how it is achieved, and what it involves are things we can understand only if we recall the Old Testament continually. Without the New Testament the Old is but a torso; and the New Testament dangles in mid-air, as it were, if one does not see its foundations in the Old. Nevertheless, it is in the New Testament that what is symbolically contained in the Old achieves its full explication and fulfilment.

Moreover, if we take our position there, we must take care not to limit ourselves to those New Testament passages which contain the term "reconciliation." The use of the term in its religious meaning is found only in Paul (Rom. 5:10, 11; 11:15; 2 Cor. 5:18-20; Eph. 2:16; Col. 1:20, 22). The word (*katallagē*, reconciliation; in German *Versöhnung*) stems from the social sector of life and refers in all these passages to the restoration of the broken relationship between God and the world, God and man (Thou, we), and God and all things. The effect of this reconciliation is repeatedly denoted by the term "peace," which may, in turn, have different meanings; for example, inner peace (of the soul) (Phil. 4:7); peace with God in the juridical sense of the word (Rom. 5:1); peace as universal restoration of the proper order on earth (Col. 1:20); and also peace as restoration of the relations among men (Eph. 2:14).

In view of the all-encompassing significance of the word "reconciliation" and of the wide range of meanings of the "peace" which issues from it, the message of reconciliation is clearly not to be limited to those texts which make explicit mention of the term. The question we are discussing is in order everywhere in the New Testament, and the entire content of the New Testament could be called a message of reconciliation. This is true of the apostolic letters, but it is equally, and more directly, true of the gospels. For this was the purpose and significance of Christ's coming: to call men back to God, to liberate the world — God's creation, according to the Old Testament — from bondage to Satan, and to restore peace on earth in the most universal sense of the word.

On the basis of this universal and central conception of the message of reconciliation I will circumscribe the specific content of this message in terms of three questions: What is its general context? What is the way or mode in which it is effected? To what extent does it affect the world today?

*   *   *

The first thing to note about the context of reconciliation is that the New Testament places it in the all-encompassing framework of the kingdom of God which was revealed in Christ's coming. Reconciliation is not just a matter between God and the individual person, but must be understood from the universal and eschatological point of view of God's coming to a world estranged from him, an advent of redemption and of judgment. In this light we must hear the call to reconciliation in the overture to the New Testament's "Repent, for the kingdom of heaven is at hand!"

Christ represents this universal character of the kingdom in many ways. At his birth the angels sang "Glory to God in the highest, and on earth peace among men with whom he is pleased." This peace is not just an inner contentment in the hearts of those who know themselves to be reconciled with God. No, it is the state of shalom, the kingdom of peace and justice of which the Psalmists had sung and which the prophets had foretold, a kingdom that begins at Christ's birth.

And so Jesus appeared among the people too. He made himself known as the one who had come to destroy the power of

Satan and all his henchmen. Christ preached the gospel in its all-embracing meaning, but he also put it into effect. When doubts beset John the Baptist so that he was not sure of Jesus and his messianic kingship, Jesus sent him the following message: "Go and tell John what you hear and see: the blind receive their sight and lame walk, lepers are cleansed and the deaf hear, and the dead are raised up, and the poor have good news preached to them" (Matt. 11:4,5). That is the peace on earth of which the angels sang in the field of Bethlehem. It cannot be denied that forgiveness of sin and reconciliation of God with man is the heart and basis of that peace, but it is no less true that forgiveness and peace involve more than the new relation between God and men and also imply a new relation among people mutually. For that reason the oppressed and afflicted, those who hunger and thirst after righteousness, are also called blessed and those who make peace are called children of God. We may conclude that reconciliation is the central focus of Jesus' universal proclamation of salvation. Only within this all-encompassing framework of the kingdom will we be able to understand the profound and true significance of reconciliation.

Some have argued that Paul has a different view of the matter. Paul is, after all, the apostle of justification by faith; and that concerns primarily the relation of the individual person to God, not one's relation to the world or interpersonal relationships. When Paul, in his well-known passage on reconciliation (2 Cor. 5:11-21) speaks of the ministry of reconciliation he refers first of all to the message of justification and of forgiveness by grace alone, which are available because God made Christ to be sin in our place "so that in him we might become the righteousness of God" (vs. 21).

Still, it would be a mistake to think that all of Paul's preaching centers on the individual's certainty of salvation. Paul's doctrine of justification is embedded in his wide perspective on the history of salvation, in which Christ's resurrection forms the great eschatological breakthrough. Therefore Paul does not exceed the limits of his own framework, when he describes Christ as the *kosmokrator* at whose feet the Father has placed all things (Eph. 1:22) and in whom all things — not only the church — acknowledge their head (Col. 1:15ff.). Therefore, the church in its activity in the world must no longer be governed by fear nor be characterized by submissiveness to the forces and rules obtaining in this world, but instead ought to be guided by faith in Christ's victory over all principalities and powers. Moreover, in this context the apostle speaks of the reconciliation of all things (Col. 1:20) (we might also render it as the "pacification" of all things), which does not refer primarily to a personal change of attitude, but to the restoration of the divine order. In other words, Paul too acknowledges the worldwide dimensions of reconciliation and sees it as a restoration of divine order in heaven and on earth, which has begun with Christ's resurrection and ascension.

There can be no doubt then that this biblical message is to be understood within the wide compass of the history of salvation and cannot be contained within some individualistic soteriology, whether that be couched in pietist or existentialist categories. This holds good not only for the preaching of Jesus and Paul but also for the entire New Testament. In Revelation the exalted Christ is repeatedly described in the language of reconciliation as the Lamb that was slain (Rev. 5:6, 8, 12, 13, etc. — 29 times in all). As such, however, he bears seven horns to symbolize his power, and we behold him before the throne of God receiving the book of the seven seals (to symbolize his lordship over the history of the future) from him who sits on the throne (Rev. 5:6). As in the gospels and the letter to the Colossians, here, too, the concept of the kingdom and the concept of reconciliation are very closely interrelated.

*   *   *

The biblical record is also pre-eminently clear and unambiguous concerning the way reconciliation is realized. If this were acknowledged in today's discussions of the subject, much would be gained. Quite simply, the way reconciliation is effected consists in the unique significance the Bible attaches to the person and work, especially the death and resurrection, of Jesus Christ as the Savior and Mediator of the world sent by God.

The decisive importance of Christ's death and resurrection in the biblical account comes to expression in various ways. As we noted, the New Testament describes reconciliation in the categories of power and dominion. Christ gains the victory over demonic powers which have set themselves up as the enemies of God. He subjects the hearts of men to himself and so restores peace, shalom. His dominion, too, is closely related to his death on the cross and his resurrection. This concept of reconciliation then depicts Christ as gaining the victory over all the powers of darkness which conspired against him, a victory gained on the cross, where he established his dominion, the power of his love and Spirit over against the power of the world. In this pattern of thought reconciliation means that the Lamb receives dominion, that the crucified and risen Christ is Lord of the cosmos, and faith in Christ is faith in his dominion.

This conception merits close attention. Still it does not exhaust the redemptive significance of Christ's death and resurrection; indeed, we may question whether it presents the most essential features of the biblical message of reconciliation. To these features we now turn.

No matter how vast and universal the context within which the Bible places reconciliation it always presents the mode by which it is effected as the way God in Christ deals with humanity. We are positioned within this vast context of past and future, of creation and redemption, of the great redemptive plan of God, of powers and demons which surpass our strength. This position determines our existence. Nevertheless, the message of reconciliation focuses above all on people and their relationship to God. The way of reconciliation through Christ's death and resurrection is also determined by that relationship and can be explained only in terms of it.

It is decisively important here that Christ took the place of the new humanity in his death and resurrection. To do that Christ had to suffer and die: it was not enough that he preached, performed miracles, and showed concern for the human condition. He also had to bear the burden of sin on the cross and in death; not just as the victim of human wickedness and ill intent, but also as the one who took on and destroyed the sin of the world as the Lamb of God. This is the most profound dimension of the Bible's message. The mode of reconciliation thus consists of more than Christ's victory and rule over demonic forces; it consists also in his willingness to be led to the slaughter as a sacrificial offering for the sins of the world.

The oldest Christian confession of reconciliation known to us is "Christ died for our sins in accordance with the scriptures" (1 Cor. 15:3). "In accordance with the scriptures" here refers to the Suffering Servant of the Lord in Isaiah 53. In other words, reconciliation (*Versöhnung, katallagē*) is effected only in the mode of expiation *(Sühnung, hilasmos)*. These words originated in a cultic context and refer to the expiatory offering, the blood of which was to cover the sins of the people. This offering was to be performed by a priest before God on behalf of the people. All of the New Testament pictures Christ's death as a sacrificial offering to God performed in our place, an offering that covers and takes away the sin of the world, reconciling us with God and calling us to be reconciled with him.

It is well known that this view of reconciliation through the blood of Christ has always encountered opposition in the history of the church; and it does so today. It is thought to be reminiscent of the heathen idea that the godhead must be appeased by means of bloody sacrifices. How — it is asked — could such a view fit in with the New Testament idea of a God of grace and love? The God of the New Testament did not have to be moved to reconciliation; he himself took the initiative and called apostate human beings back to communion with him. And so, some have reinterpreted the sacrifice of Christ, for example by claiming that Christ delivered himself to death in order to bring us to remorse and repentance, which in their turn would serve to reconcile us with God (the so-called subjective theory of reconciliation).

No matter how much Christ's death ought to bring *us* to repentance and conversion, it is no less necessary in order to cover and take away the sin of the world, as an offering of expiation which he as the great high priest had to perform before God — not to move God to different ideas, not to alter his mood, for God himself took the initiative to give us his Son for a holy peace offering. But God's love does not reduce the need for sin to be covered by the blood of reconciliation. God forgives the sinner, but he does not make room for sin. Sin must be displayed in its reprehensible character, and God must carry sin to judgment. Since sin cannot stand before his countenance, he must execute judgment on it. In this execution Christ took our place, and so God himself has restored the broken relationship with us. That is why Paul can say that we were reconciled with God (on Golgotha) *while we were yet sinners* (Rom. 5:8); that is why Christ says concerning himself that he came to give his life as a ransom for many; and that is why we are called again and again to the Lord's supper to commemorate the sacrifice he performed for us and in our place before God. He speaks of his body and of his blood in sacrificial terms: his body was given over to death on our behalf and his blood was poured out for us as an expiation for all our sins.

This meaning of Christ's self-sacrifice provides the New Testament message of reconciliation with a depth-dimension of which the church may never lose sight. To slight this dimension is to lose touch with the very mystery of the gospel. It is hardly surprising, therefore, that many who live out of this mystery of salvation and who find there the only consolation for life and death view with suspicion any new ideas putting all the emphasis on what *our* lives ought to reveal, instead of emphasizing what *Christ* has done, once and for all, in our place. Is this not a radical shift in focus? And ought we not rather to count as nothing all human effort so that we focus our attention and faith exclusively on what Christ, by his death and resurrection, has fully done, once and for all all, in our place?

To think that way is to run the risk of making a serious mistake. For although we are completely correct to stress the expiatory and atoning effect of Christ's sacrifice as the focal point of the biblical account of reconciliation, we may not restrict the power of that sacrifice to what Christ once suffered and performed in our place. We refer again to the victorious power of Christ's death and resurrection in his battle against the powers and demons which, as God's adversaries, chained persons to their service. But this victory not only affects Satan and his subjects; the suffering and death of Christ also exert a liberating and renewing power in the lives of all who believe in him. The effect of this sacrifice is not only that it frees us from the guilt and punishment of sin, but also that it subjects us to Christ's regime. Reconciliation means that the world — all things, man included — is again put right with God. To that end man must be freed from the *guilt* of sin through the *blood* of Christ as well as from the *power* of sin through the *Spirit* of Christ.

The biblical message of reconciliation is full of God. It is also full of man, but only from God's point of view (*sub specie Dei*). Human life cannot find fulfilment in itself, nor in the I-thou relation to the neighbor, nor in the overwhelming, God-given instrumentation of life, of knowledge and wisdom and development, but only in communion with him who said: "I am the Way, the Truth and the Life: no one comes to the Father but by me."

* * *

As to the question of the *extent* to which reconciliation affects the world today, we have to recall that the biblical message of reconciliation has a universal scope, and we may not reduce it to the strict personal relation between God and the individual human being. God's reconciliation also affects our relations. Just as love of God and love of neighbor are closely related in the twofold commandment of love, so it is in the biblical message of reconciliation. By reconciling us to himself, God also puts us in a new relationship to the world about us, a relationship no longer governed by fear and hostility but by peace and love towards God. This renewed relation must not be understood merely as a consequence of reconciliation with God, but is itself part and parcel of it. In Ephesians Paul says that Christ has broken down the hostility between Jews and Gentiles and has thus become our peace, that is, he is the peace *among us*. Reconciliation with God institutes peace among humans, since they partake of the same redemption. The same thing is expressed in the well-known words of Colossians 3:11, which leave all religious, social, and racial discrimination far behind as having been removed in Christ: "Where there cannot be Greek and Jew, circumcised and uncircumcised, barbarian, Scythian, slave, free man, but Christ is all, and in all" (cf. Gal. 3:28).

Undoubtedly these passages refer first of all to relationships *within the church.* One may not use these texts to proclaim a so-called objective unity of the human race supposedly established with the coming of Christ, a unity from which we are to proceed as a given of faith. For the major condition for such a shared unity, after all, is reconciliation with God. Nevertheless, it is of paramount significance that reconciliation with God aims at and serves to transcend and do away with all manner of discrimination among people. It is important in this connection that the record of reconciliation repeatedly makes explicit mention of the world as the object of divine action: "in Christ God was reconciling the world to himself" (2 Cor. 5:19) and "God so loved the world" (John 3:16). Here again we are not to think of some objective universal atonement (whether a person is aware of it or not, and whether he believes it or not) but to think of the grace of God who comes to all without distinction, who wants to give eternal life to "everyone who believes."

This should motivate the church to show proof of that same all-embracing will to peace and reconciliation in its attitude to the world. This theme is stressed particularly in the pastoral letters (1 and 2 Timothy and Titus), which constantly appeal to the universal character of divine reconciliation. In 1 Timothy 2 the church is exhorted to make prayerful intercession "for *all men*," also for kings and those in high places in order that there may be peace. For this is how God, who (as we read elsewhere in Timothy) seeks the redemption of *all* and wants *all* to know of this redemption, would have it. It is curious — and useful for the formation of our thought — that here the political and social dimensions, too, are drawn within the compass of reconciliation. The letter to Titus also expresses this idea. Those who believe are called to be gentle, showing meekness to *all* (3:2). After all, they themselves used to live in malice and envy toward each other, but they have been liberated through the coming of God's mercy and love of man (*philanthropia*). The faithful may not occupy a negative or isolated position with respect to social and political relationships, but must instead prove themselves to be ready and willing to serve, "submissive to rulers and authorities . . . obedient . . . ready for any honest work" (Titus 3:1).

It is along these lines that we must understand the idea to which we have referred several times, that God was in Christ in order to reconcile all things to himself, as the letter to the Colossians puts it. It is not easy to fathom this far-reaching thought in its full meaning. That it was said to the church in Colossae is not without reason. The church in Colossae was a church intimidated by human philosophy, by the principles and the taboos of this world and the demonic powers suspected to be behind them. To such a church it was said: God "has delivered us from the dominion of darkness and transferred us to the kingdom of his beloved Son. . . . Through him [he has reconciled] to himself all things . . . making peace by the blood of his cross" (3:13, 20). And so the apostle concludes — and we see here how far reconciliation does affect the world in which we live — If you died with Christ to the principles of this world, why do you live as though you still belonged to the world? Why do you submit to the dogmas, the institutions, the taboos, the enchantments of this world? This is a tremendously bold and courageous word to the church: Do not submit yourself to the world, do not believe in any spiritual power except Christ, not only on the personal level but also on the cultural and social levels. I am not one of those who only criticize the existing order, existing institutions, established authority, because I believe in order, in legal systems, even in existing legal systems. But I also believe that human society can be and is caught in the clutch of pernicious institutions, moral and social prejudices, unjust distribution of power and wealth. The church is told that it especially, as the church of Jesus Christ, should not believe in those powers as inevitable structures, just belonging to this world and therefore to be accepted for the time being. The breakthrough of the kingdom of God in history means also the proclamation of that spiritual freedom and the mandate not to acquiesce to what is essentially wrong but is often glibly referred to as a matter of "historical necessity."

Therefore, when we hear the gospel, go and teach the nations to observe all that Christ has commanded, we have to be aware that the *full* message of reconciliation is at stake: reconciliation by the blood of Christ saving souls from the guilt of sin; but also reconciliation by the power of Christ. And this has something to do with that reconciliation of all things; that is, it also applies to dimensions of life and human existence greater than the personal. The church as a whole has perhaps thought too much and too long in the categories of the two realms, the realm of Christ, applicable only to the church and personal life, and the realm of the world for the other aspects of life. This has often obscured the totalitarian character of the kingdom of God and reconciliation. A double conversion, so to speak, is necessary, just as the great commandment of love is a double commandment.

Then, undoubtedly, the danger exposes itself again that the "second" conversion and second commandment become the whole thing; as people say that God is only met and only served in our neighbor and that the actual meaning of reconciliation is thus to be understood in the social sense of the word. But this distortion of the message of reconciliation may never be a pretext for the church to limit its interest in this message to our relationship to God and to the content of the first commandment.

Even then not all has been said about the all-embracing power and extent of reconciliation. For the reconciliation of all things, as achieved in the cross of Jesus Christ, does not only mean that there is room to live and a calling to work for the church in the present world, but also that the world itself, even in its present state, is the object of God's redemptive will and work. Christ, therefore, is the hope of the world in this all-encompassing sense of the word.

Without a doubt this is complex and difficult to understand and explain. It includes the powerful "objective" fact that the future of the world does not belong to the devil but to the Lord, and that therefore the world even in its most desperate (and sinful) situations is not abandoned to the power of darkness. But it also contains a "subjective" element: the world itself has a certain awareness, an intimation, a feeling or whatever you want to call it, of that salvation which is in Christ and of being liberated from the powers of darkness. Paul in Romans 8 calls that the groaning of the entire creation for the revealing of the sons of God. Of course this does not mean that the world is consciously and purposely waiting for the return of Christ, for it does not do that. But in its struggle for liberation, for justice, for truth, and for peace the world unconsciously witnesses to this reconciliation of all things. That is why Paul says that creation is *waiting* for the revealing of the sons of God. In the context of Romans 8, this looks forward to the great future, but it also applies to the revealing of the sons of God in *this* world. Jeşus himself points to it in his Sermon on the Mount, when he says: "Let your light so shine before men, that they may see your good works and give glory to your Father who is in heaven" (Matt. 5:16). This presupposes that there is a knowledge of God in the world, which in the midst of all sin and misery still keeps alive the hope of a better world. Paul especially points time and again to this remnant of awareness of God in the world. God not only discloses his wrath from heaven on increasing human apostasy (Rom. 1); he continues to write his law on the hearts of those who do not know him in Christ (Rom. 2). If I understand the apostle correctly, he describes in a still more poignant way in Romans 7 the spiritual struggle of the man beyond Christ, the struggle of one who is indeed enslaved to sin, but who still knows the law, who knows and wants a better life, and who therefore wrestles with the help of the law and of moral ideals for real humanness and for a better world. And yet he always fails because he wants to be saved through that law and through those ideals and not through grace.

We also have to keep those things in mind when we speak of the extent of reconciliation and of the kingship of Christ in the world and in history. The world is not without hope, not without messianic longing, even though it does not know the name "under heaven given among men by which we must be saved" (Acts 4:12). This is also an important indication for the church as to how it should stand in the world. It does not exist to condemn all that is in the world. For in this world, the light of God, the light of the sun, of truth and justice also shines. It shines with interrupted rays, because it is always obscured by the clouds of sin and unbelief. Nevertheless, we should not underestimate that light. The world itself witnesses unknowingly in all sorts of ways that it is not of the devil but of God. This is no little thing; on the contrary, it can and may be a tremendous help in the struggle for a better world, for peace, and for righteousness. It can help prepare and open the way to Christ himself.

But *here, in Christ,* is where the great decision lies for man and for the world. That which is good and beautiful and true in the world cannot by itself open up the way to the kingdom, nor can it bring history to its completion and fulfilment. Paul does not speak about it in that way either. He instead points in a surpassing way to the bankruptcy of all the attempts of human persons and of the world, of Israel and the nations, to find the way to the future by way of human idealism or legalistic diligence or pagan humanism. Indeed — more strongly put — even that which is best and most noble in man clearly reveals that the world cannot save itself; for *Christ* is the light of the world, and the way of that light is the way of the cross. *Via lucis, via crucis.* There is no other name. That is the stumbling-block of the gospel: reconciliation is in him and from him, and all other ways to realize the messianic dream are dead ends.

In a certain way this is a harsh truth, and the church always is being tempted to abandon something of it. But it has no other choice than to confess that name which is above all names, because every knee must bow before him. The reconciliation of all things is not anonymous, the kingdom is not an *it*, an ideal, a dream, but it is a *he*. That is how God deals with us. Ultimately it is a matter of our subjection, of bowing our knees before him. For reconciliation is from above and not from men; it is out of grace and not by works. If the church were to practice *this* in the sight of the world, it would do more than it could do by anything else. The church does not exist to condemn the world. But its solidarity with the world can never go so far that it no longer confronts the world with the choice, with the decision, with respect to the cross and to that one name which is given under heaven.

With that message of reconciliation the church was once sent into history; and that is still its task in history until the present day. The church got no timetable from the Lord by which to read the hour of history, nor did it receive a divine plan about the course history would follow. But the task of the church is quite clear. Not to remain where it is, nor to remain self-involved, but to go forth, meeting the future, until he comes and history is discharged into the kingdom of God and the full reconciliation of all things.

6.

Jesus and Apocalyptic

THE SUBJECT of this essay has taken on new priority in recent developments in church and theology. This is not the first time this has happened. Again and again apocalyptic disturbs the peace in the exegesis of the New Testament; especially when it comes in the form of the question "What is the *relevance* of apocalyptic for the faith of the church?"

Since the days of Albert Schweitzer and Johannes Weiss (as a matter of fact even earlier) New Testament scholars have known that the preaching and appearance of Jesus of Nazareth have to be understood against the background of Old Testament and late Jewish eschatology. During the ascendancy of "liberal" theology little was made, in a theological sense, of this background, which was perceived as "fantastic." The attempt was made to leave eschatology in the background as much as possible and to present the preaching of Jesus as a breakthrough into this apocalyptic framework. The change came during the period after the First World War, when humanity awoke from its dream of eternal progress. Serious efforts were made to let the eschatological emphasis of the New Testament message in general and of the preaching of Jesus in particular come into its own.

This then led to a new understanding of the concept "eschatology," an interpretation directed not to the "horizontal" course of history to the end-time, nor to the how or the when of the end-time, but rather to the actual situation in which the individual sees himself placed, when confronted with the message that the end of all things is near. The theological meaning of New Testament eschatology would not lie in the knowledge of the future and of the end of history, but in the actual decision before which the new future of God continually places us here and now. This is the well-known existentialistic interpretation of eschatology, in which in the field of New Testament research the name of Rudolf Bultmann is prominent. This existentialistic interpretation of eschatology meant at the same time the so-called demythologizing of the apocalyptic frame of the New Testament message. According to Bultmann apocalypticism is the mythological expression of the way man understood himself in history. It is this existentialistic self-understanding which counts in New Testament apocalypticism. The rest of it is only mythology and religious fantasy.[1]

Closed and consistent, this program of demythologizing and existentialistic interpretation of apocalyptic influenced the study of New Testament theology for a long time. In recent years, however, doubts have risen on a large scale about the legitimacy of this interpretation. As often has been the case in the history of exegesis, the text and the evidence of Scripture appear stronger than the framework into which its interpreters, on the basis of their specific anthropological or philosophical presuppositions, have wanted to press it. If it is true, as has been admitted by Bultmann, that the "setting" of the New Testament kerygma has an eschatological character; and if it is also true that this eschatology in its New Testament form has been strongly influenced by Jewish apocalypticism, then it may seriously be questioned whether one can give the kerygma such an exclusively existentialistic and individualistic interpretation as have Bultmann and his followers. For does the specific meaning of apocalypticism not in fact lie in its concern for the counsel of God with regard to *all things* and its intention, in close conjunction with the Old Testament prophecy, to bring back the whole world and all that is created under the kingship of God?

The decline of Bultmann's influence has coincided with the increasing interest of recent systematic theology in the course and the future of history, as for instance in the theology of hope of Jürgen Moltmann and the historical views of Wolfhart Pannenberg. There is a strong regression in the interest in existentialism, insofar as it concentrates itself on individual man. I refer, for instance, to the severe criticism of Bultmann by Dorothee Sölle. All the emphasis is now laid on social and political conditions as decisive for the position of the human being in history. The biblical message of salvation is consequently explained as a message of liberation from unrighteousness and discrimination in the social and political sense of the word. And all this is placed in the light of the great eschatological expectation of salvation. This partly explains the new interest in the apocalyptic character of the message of Jesus. Attention is directed to the future, when the poor will inherit the earth and all who are hungry and thirsty for righteousness will be satisfied.

This new interest in New Testament eschatology and apocalypticism raises new questions of its own. In how far can the progress of history be connected to the coming of the eschatological kingdom of God? Does apocalypticism not just mean the end of history, as Bultmann always pointed out, and therefore in fact not allow any more room for a perspective about the future of this present world and of the development of society? Still, no matter how one wants to judge these perspectives, it cannot be denied, particularly with respect to Jesus' preaching of the nearness of the kingdom, that hermeneutic attempts to undo the New Testament kerygma of its cosmic world- and future-enclosing dimensions are out of favor in current theology.

This shift in theological interest may explain why apocalypticism has received immense attention in the New Testament research. Even in the Bultmannian school, opposition to a one-sided existentialistic interpretation of the kerygma has become stronger and stronger. Ernst Käsemann has argued strongly that the kingship of Christ in the New Testament is not limited to personal salvation but that it has cosmic dimensions too. One cannot remove this central notion from the message of the New Testament without seriously diminishing and changing that message. In this respect the apocalyptic interpretation of the person and the work of Christ in early Christianity is, according to Käsemann, essential for understanding the New Testament. That is how he arrived at his much-quoted pronouncement that apocalyptic is the mother of Christian theology.[2]

True, Käsemann is of the opinion (and in this he reminds one of the old liberal tradition) that this apocalyptic character should be denied to Christ's own proclamation. While the preaching of John the Baptist moves entirely in this apocalyptic framework, Christ would have disassociated himself in this from his predecessor. The early church, however, under the influence of charismatic, prophetic voices in their midst, understood the works and the person of Jesus in the light of Jewish apocalyptic expectation, particularly by identifying him with the Son of Man of Daniel 7. And, Käsemann says, from their point of view they could not have done better. For in one sense or another you have to have this all-embracing, cosmic dimension in your Christian message. And Christian theology without this expectation of the full lordship of Christ over all things can never be complete and legitimate.

Not surprisingly some have accused Käsemann of a real inconsistency in his position. His view of the preaching of Jesus necessitates a "double discontinuity," on the one side with the apocalyptic preaching of John the Baptist and on the other side with the apocalyptic interpretations and expectations of the early Christian community. Would this not mean that Jesus' own preaching took place in a sort of historical vacuum? And how could the later church have identified Jesus with the Son of Man in Daniel, if they could not find a clear point of contact with it in Jesus' self-revelation? Could they rely for such an identification only on "prophetic voices" in their midst? What do we actually know of such a boom of charismatic apocalypticism in the early Christian church? Does it not make much more sense, even on historical grounds, to understand Jesus' own preaching as apocalyptic in itself? Nonetheless, Käsemann's acknowledgment of the essential significance of New Testament apocalypticism, and his vigorous defense of this position against the sharp attacks this evoked from many of his old friends, illustrates that the apocalyptic dimensions of the New Testament message cannot convincingly be touched up by modern criticism. That this must have its consequences for the interpretation of Jesus' own preaching cannot, in my opinion, finally be denied. The book by the German scholar Klaus Koch, *Ratlos von der Apokalyptik* (1970) ("Desperate about Apocalypticism") is illustrative in this connection. Koch's fascinating review shows how in the course of biblical research the attempt is always made to reduce the theme and value of apocalypticism as much as possible in the New Testament kerygma, especially in the preaching of Jesus, but how it has again and again appeared necessary to return to it. Theology is in a sense desperate in the face of the apocalyptic character of the New Testament message, but at the same time it has to accept it in order correctly to reflect the preaching of Jesus and the New Testament kerygma built on it.

* * *

Now it may be remarked with some justification that to these questions no clear answer can be given until there is a clear definition of what is meant by apocalypticism. Is it in fact possible to speak in general of "apocalyptic"? It is well known that what we call apocalypticism is a complex phenomenon both in its forms and its content. It found its expression in a form of literature which in the Bible is rooted in the last books of the Old Testament, most clearly in the book of Daniel, but also with unmistakable points of contact in the older prophecies.[3] It developed for a long time in late Judaism and led an independent existence in it, though the place and influence of apocalypticism in the spiritual life of Jewish people in those days are anything but clear to us.

Apocalyptic is characterized by a dramatic-symbolic manner of describing the future. It occurs especially in the form of visions similar to what we find in the New Testament Apocalypse of John, whence the name for the literary genre was later borrowed. These visions contain very remarkable material — images, representations, forms, and symbols — which also occurs in non-visionary passages. Their meaning is often far from transparent, and sometimes they make a fantastic impression on us. Yet most scholars are convinced that apocalypticism is not born of abstract speculations about the future. Behind apocalypticism lie totally different forces: the desire of and the urge of the human spirit to rise above the misery, mystery, and contradictions of history, and to seek a solution for this in the presently hidden, but soon-to-be-expected, completion and culmination of the divine plan. To discover that plan, the long eras of history were examined and categorized into periods. The writers identified themselves with the great figures of the past — Enoch, the patriarchs, Moses, Isaiah, Baruch, Ezra — in order to present in the form of a prophecy what was regarded by them to be the last chapter of history, as the outcome of a process that had long since been coming to fulfilment.

Obviously this is only a brief characterization of a very complicated phenomenon. No less important than the forms and structures is the apocalyptic view of life and history. All important in this respect is in fact the scheme of the two worlds or aeons — the *"aeōn mellōn"* and the *"aeōn houtos,"* which in the strictest sense are opposed to each other, as the old and the new, the evil and the divine world, and which seem to have nothing in common and no other continuity except that both are taken up in the counsel of God.

Closely related is the spiritual concentration of apocalypticism on the imminent end of this world and the ardently expected dawn of the coming world. In addition the universal and cosmic framework in which apocalypticism sees history being taken up causes all human certainties to disappear and throws man back for his salvation more and more on himself and his own personal relation to God. In this context the relation of apocalypticism to ethics comes into the discussion: the question of whether or not a pessimistic and deterministic character would be typical of apocalypticism in an anthropological and ethical sense. All these questions are important for judging the lasting meaning and relevance of apocalypticism as a particular specimen of the eschatological way of thinking.

* * *

If we return to our special theme, Jesus and apocalypticism, it becomes clear immediately that the form and presentation of the preaching of Jesus as it comes to us in the gospels are quite different from what is characteristic of the Jewish apocalyptic way of thinking. If one sets the obscure and inscrutable visions, the fantastic representations and calculations, of many intertestamental apocalypses next to the commandments, parables, and proverbs of Jesus in the Sermon on the Mount and elsewhere, one can ask whether there even is a point of comparison. But also if we try to qualify the more future-oriented predictions of Jesus, his warnings and penitential preaching with regard to the future, we cannot simply categorize these under what we know, for example, from the book of Daniel or from the Apocalypse of John.

Here lies one of the reasons many scholars have insisted that Jesus moved consciously away from the later apocalyptic development of prophecy and returned to the great prophetic tradition of the Old Testament, of whom Deutero-Isaiah is the last. But can one thus place the background of Jesus' preaching about four to five centuries earlier? For, though it may be correct to place emphasis on the relationship between the gospels and the older prophecies, the later development of prophecy (for example, in the book of Daniel) is also visible in the preaching of Jesus. And that line of prophecy also characterizes late Jewish apocalypticism. This is the sort of prophecy in which the expectation of salvation shifts itself more and more from this world to the coming world, with its universalistic perspective, its image of the imminent end of the world and the day of God's judgment, in which the whole cosmos is involved.

Undoubtedly, the roots of this expectation are grounded in the older prophecy, with the result that a clear separation of prophecy and apocalyptic, as advocated by some, is totally impossible. But there does exist, in the concentration on the passing of this present world and the imminent dawning of the new, an indication of a specifically apocalyptic view of the future. Without this background the New Testament in its totality and the preaching of Jesus in particular cannot be understood, no matter how unique and independent these may be in comparison with late Jewish apocalypticism. This is true not only of the great discourse in Mark 13, sometimes styled, perhaps not unjustly, as the "small" or "synoptic" apocalypse, but also of the overture of the whole gospel, the proclamation with which Jesus came to the people of Israel: "The time is fulfilled, and the kingdom of God is at hand; repent, and believe in the gospel" (Mark 1:15). And it holds especially for the most significant self-appellation, designated to Jesus by the univocal tradition, namely, *Son of Man.* It is important to go a little deeper into these two central concepts: *kingdom of God* and *Son of Man.*

Jesus' preaching on the *kingdom of God* brings our discussion to a very crucial point. On the one side, it cannot be denied that this concept "kingdom of heaven" was derived from the late Jewish expectation of the future. This implies, however, that Jesus saw his whole preaching and mission in the framework of the great future as promised by God, proclaimed by the prophets, and expected by Israel; and one cannot separate this concept from its historical roots without distorting it. This means that with the coming of the kingdom as announced by Jesus everything in heaven and on earth is involved, not only the individual person but also history — the whole cosmos, as is already evident from the third petition of the Lord's Prayer. On the other hand, it can no less be denied that Jesus' preaching of the kingdom fundamentally shatters the framework of Jewish apocalypticism.

Even the preaching of John the Baptist with regard to the imminence of the kingdom of God receives in the interpretation, and in the ministry of Jesus, a decisive shift in emphasis, which was unintelligible to John. This shift is this, that Jesus proclaimed the kingdom of God not in the first place as a cosmic revolution of all things but as a spiritual reality which comes to man in his words, deeds, and forgiveness of sin, and which is therefore present already in *this* world. This means that the kingdom of God became a reality in a totally different way from what was expected in Jewish apocalypticism. It derives its character from the self-revelation of the earthly Jesus (which, for example, should be explained in connection with his parables) and is revealed by him particularly in the passion and death God laid on him. That is the uniqueness of the kingdom of God as proclaimed and presented by Jesus.

This, however, does not mean the renunciation of the great future of the kingdom of God as proclaimed by the prophets and expected by Israel. In all that Jesus said and did and bestowed, the future of the kingdom is in the picture, too. Present and future in the preaching of Jesus exist in an unbreakable relationship and are in the most absolute sense interdependent. In the proclamations of the coming of the kingdom (for example, in the Sermon on the Mount) the present and future continually alternate with one another; and it is often not easy to see both in correct relationship to one another. All the parables speak of the future of the kingdom, though their meaning is already directed to the present; and all the miracles, too, are directed to the future. The presentation of the kingdom in the present is in many ways to be understood only as a sign and anticipation of the future. That also holds for the person of Jesus. He is "the coming one," the eschatological figure who was heralded by John. But he can still be misunderstood today. "Blessed is he who takes no offense at me" (Matt. 11:6). That is why Jesus continues to speak of the future of the kingdom. And when he does that, all things in heaven and on earth are involved. He does not only speak of the future restoration of the kingdom of David, but in apocalyptic language of the redemption and judgment which will include the whole world and the whole cosmos. And that is not only true of the much-discussed apocalyptic discourse of Mark 13, but also forms the visible or presupposed background of all the pronouncements of Jesus about the future (e.g., Matt. 5:18; 8:11,12; 10:15; 13:30,43; Mark 10:30; 12:25, etc.).

All this stands out more clearly when we include Jesus' pronouncements about the *Son of Man* in our examination. For our theme this name is of particular importance. Its use in fact provides a direct relation, at least in a few pronouncements, with Daniel 7 and the apocalyptic figure who appears there, who is clothed with all power by the "Ancient of days" (Mark 14:62; Matt. 28:18). Therefore it is especially the interpretation of this name "Son of Man" which is of decisive significance with regard to the nature of the preaching of Jesus and of his self-revelation.

The gospel pronouncements about the Son of Man are the subject of much recent theological discussion. According to a number of scholars, one should deny all of these pronouncements to Jesus. Professor Vielhauer, for instance, contends that there would be a real incongruity between the non-apocalyptic way in which Jesus preached the kingdom and the apocalyptical sayings concerning the Son of Man.[4] The latter, therefore, should not be considered genuine sayings of Jesus himself but ascribed to the early church. And we saw already that Käsemann, though much more in favor of apocalypticism than Vielhauer, is nevertheless convinced that not Jesus himself but the church of Jerusalem understood him in the light of apocalypticism and that therefore the church and not Jesus himself made the identification with the Son of Man of Daniel 7. And the church did this, as Käsemann says, under the strong influence of the charismatic and prophetic voices in their midst.

Now it cannot be denied on the basis of comparison of the

synoptic gospels that the title Son of Man has undergone a sort of expansion in the early tradition. While for instance Matthew speaks of the Son of Man, Mark or Luke in the same sayings may speak of "I" or "me." This is a clear indication that the development of the tradition has multiplied the use of the name Son of Man.[5]

But it is another thing to deny to Jesus every use of this name. This cannot be done without doing violence to the evidence. As Colpe has pointed out in his well-known article on the Son of Man,[6] a very close relationship existed between the concepts kingdom of heaven and Son of Man. Daniel 7 speaks not only of the Son of Man but also of the kingdom of God. Kingdom of God and Son of Man are in a certain sense parallel concepts. It would be most arbitrary to ascribe to Jesus the idea of the kingdom of God but to deny to him the use of the name Son of Man.

Secondly, the fact that the title Son of Man in the New Testament comes almost exclusively from the mouth of the historical Jesus and hardly seems to have played a role in the later church, is a very strong argument against the assertion that the title Son of Man for Jesus would have originated in the early church.

Even Bultmann does not want to go so far as to deny to Jesus every use of the name Son of Man. But he does argue that the fact that Jesus speaks only in the third person about the Son of Man proves that he did not identify himself with the Son of Man, but referred to a future apocalyptic figure whom he still expected. And it was only the later church who identified Jesus himself with this figure.[7] But this opinion is dubious, for the authority with which Jesus acted and spoke, as the one sent by God (Matt. 5:21ff.; Luke 11:20; 17:20) hardly comports with the idea that he regarded himself only as a predecessor and not as the ultimate Savior.

Still, many find it difficult to believe that Jesus would have identified himself with the apocalyptic Son of Man of Daniel 7. Schweizer argues in his commentary on Mark that this name was originally derived not from Daniel 7, but from the prophecies of Ezekiel, where God speaks to the prophet as "child of man." That would mean that the name Son of Man was an indication of Jesus' humility, not his apocalyptic exaltation. Now it cannot be denied that Jesus often speaks in the gospels of the humble state of the Son of Man; for example when he says that he has no place to lay his head (Matt. 8:20). But that this name originates with Ezekiel rather than with Daniel is unacceptable. Nowhere in the gospels do we have indications that there exists such an essential relationship between Jesus and Ezekiel, while in a number of instances the relationship with Daniel is clearly evident.

Finally there is the idea that the expression originally had no prophetic and apocalyptic implications at all, but simply meant "man," and was used by Jesus to express his solidarity with the people. This interpretation, elaborated by the Norwegian scholar Ragnar Leivestadt,[8] goes so far as to reject the idea that this name in Daniel and Enoch was meant to be a term of glory, and sees it there, too, as an indication of a human-like figure. So the term would have in Jesus' mouth only the meaning "man," a synonym for "I," but as qualification of this the particular meaning of a mere man, a man among men.

Regardless of how one interprets the meaning of the expression in Daniel 7, it is undeniable that this figure is invested with great power. Nor can it be denied that in Enoch and certainly also in the gospel, the name Son of Man is brought in direct relation with Daniel 7 and thus with the figure invested with all power. That is why it is difficult to see how one could deny that the use of this name in connection with Daniel 7 would qualify the bearer of his name as an apocalyptic figure.

Out of all these often laborious and confused discussions about the Son of Man, amid all that is uncertain, two things came to the fore: first, that on purely historical grounds the use of this name by Jesus, in close relationship to his own person, can hardly be denied; and second, that Jesus has put himself in direct relationship with the figure invested with power in the apocalyptic prophecy of Daniel.

This obviously does not mean, however, that the term Son of Man is reserved exclusively for statements which speak of the future glory of the Son of Man. We must rather point out that the totally unique and sovereign way Jesus spoke about the kingdom of God also holds for his use of the name Son of Man. As the kingdom of God is not merely future in the preaching of Jesus, but has already become a present divine reality, so also it can be said of the Son of Man that he has the power and authority *on earth* — here and now — to forgive sins (Matt. 9:6); and just as the kingdom of God has a paradoxical form of existence, hidden from human eyes and attacked by hostile powers (Matt. 13:4,5,13), so also there are paradoxical pronouncements about the Son of Man. He has no place to lay his head (Matt. 8:20). Above all, the Son of Man must suffer much (Mark 8:31). Certainly this "must" clearly belongs to fixed "apocalyptic" terminology (Rev. 1:1); and it needs no further argument here that this "must" flows forth from the divine counsel of God, not merely from the wickedness of the people. Nevertheless, the statement that the Son of Man must suffer remains highly paradoxical. For "Son of Man" like "kingdom of God" is by its very nature a *terminus gloriae.* And that notion of glory comes to the fore also in Jesus' sayings about the Son of Man, in complete analogy with what is said about the future of the kingdom. Some day the prophecy of Daniel 7 will be fulfilled, and then the Son of Man will appear in divine glory (Matt. 13:26), suddenly and unexpectedly (Matt. 24:27). He himself will sit on the throne of God (Luke 22:69) and send out his angels (Matt. 13:27) and pronounce judgment on the earth and its people (Matt. 19:28; 25:31). In these pronouncements the Son of Man is also called "the king" (Matt. 25:31ff.). One can say that in this respect the sayings about the Son of Man bring to expression in a personal and therefore explicit manner what is implicitly said in the preaching of the kingdom about the person of Jesus. For the person of Jesus is also the secret of the kingdom whose coming Jesus has proclaimed.

*   *   *

We face here the issue — for us inscrutable and inexplicable — of the self-consciousness of Jesus. That Jesus identified himself with the apocalyptical figure of the Son of Man may seem strange to us. But we cannot remove this grand and lofty strangeness from Jesus' words without great arbitrariness and bias. We cannot cut the historical figure of Jesus down to our own size and ascribe to the later church anything that seems strange to us, in order to be able to distance ourselves from it more easily. This strangeness holds not only for the special apocalyptic name and presentation Jesus applied to himself, but it holds for the total way he understood and presented himself to Israel. He placed his whole mission in and related it to the framework of Israel's expectation of the great future, and he used the language of Jewish apocalyptic for this.

This means, too, that we have always to keep in mind the special character of the apocalyptic way of speaking. In the prophecy of Daniel the Son of Man is just a symbol, not the designation of a historical personality. Therefore it is not without reason that Jesus speaks of the Son of Man exclusively in the third person. He maintained in this way a certain distance between his own personality and the figure of the Son of Man. Perhaps one may say that the way Jesus was speaking of the Son of Man is actually more an indication of his divine authority now and in the future than a direct self-identification with the Son of Man. It means that what had been proclaimed until now in prophetic symbols and images has become, in *his* coming and in his person, a new and unexpected reality and will become reality. This was the way in which Jesus made prophetic apocalypticism relevant to his disciples.

Speaking about this relevance, I realize that the less inclined we are to ascribe the apocalyptic sayings to the early church rather than Jesus himself, the more we face the real problem raised by the title of Rowley's 1947 book *The Relevance of Apocalyptic*. We must reckon with the possibility that Jesus may appear more strange to us as he comes nearer to us, stranger in the grand and lofty transcendence to which he lays claim, stranger, too, in the historical conceptual framework in which he expressed himself to his contemporaries. It cannot be the task of theological exegesis to retouch this strangeness as much as possible. Even to theologians the saying applies: "Blessed is he who takes no offense in me." On the other hand, one should not deny that theological explanation is bound to make the Scriptures understandable for present readers and present hearers, even though the individual exegete will be convinced that his efforts to add to the understanding of the greatness and strangeness of Jesus will always remain inadequate.

* * *

With this in mind, the following points seem to me of fundamental importance.

1. In every interpretation of Jesus' preaching two things must always get their rightful place: first, that this preaching of the kingdom and its attendant relation to the coming of the Son of Man is only to be understood against the background of the Old Testament and later Jewish apocalypticism; and second, that Jesus, in a totally unique and sovereign manner, gave these concepts their content, so that the key to the understanding should not be sought in one or another apocalyptic scheme, but in the preaching of Jesus.

2. With regard to the *time* of the kingdom Jesus, contrary to the current idea of "apocalyptic," proclaims the kingdom not only as future but also in his coming and work as an already present reality. In Jesus' apocalyptic preaching the human being is not only referred to the future for salvation, but also to the presence of the grace of God, to the freedom and the calling to live out of this new beginning as a child of God. All this brings with it an unmistakably different mentality with respect to this "evil" aeon. As Jesus goes out to seek the lost sheep of Israel and to orient himself, with the full power of God's grace, to all who have no helper, so he also asks his

disciples to be the salt of the earth and the light of the world
as children of God. Instead of the mostly negative mentality
with regard to this world which one finds in the apocalyptic
literature, Jesus comes with a positive approach. The meaning
of this is therefore so radical and unlimited in its effect, because it is supported by the universality of the kingdom of
God, as a reign of grace and righteousness.

3. It can be rightly concluded that the kingdom, as in-
augurated by Jesus, includes history also. This is not only to
be understood in the sense of the apocalyptic tradition, namely, that the coming of the kingdom forms the conclusion and
the outcome of bygone history. Fulfilment which came with
Jesus does not only mean the end of history. The kingdom of
God also enters in a new and unprecedented way into the onward stream of history, as "a new doctrine imbued with
power," a "seed," "salt," "light," "new wine" in old wineskins
— a newness which like that of the kingdom of God breaks all
boundaries, affects all relationships (cf. Matt. 13:8, 31, 33).

4. Still, there remains in Jesus' preaching a real tension
between the *present* and the *future* of the kingdom and of the
Son of Man. This tension does not allow itself to be released
within the boundaries of this aeon. There remains an antithesis
between what Augustine called the City of God and the City
of Man. We see nowhere that Jesus anticipates a process of
development in which the old, "evil" world will be gradually
changed into the kingdom of God. Nowhere have the disciples
received a mandate to complete the victory of Christ. The
character of faith and of hope which Jesus kindled in the
hearts of his disciples is of a different nature from that of an
optimistic cultural view. It is a new assurance, concentrated
in the person of Christ, of the presence of the mercy of God
and of his redeeming righteousness in the midst of and in
spite of everything that seems to contradict this in the present.
In the death and resurrection of Christ this assurance receives
its unexpected confirmation in both directions: in spite of the
power of darkness, which tends to extinguish the brightest

light, and *in* this power, God in Christ is present in the world to open the way to his future.

Not that one should interpret the tension between present and future of the kingdom as Bultmann does, in an exclusively individualistic manner, for example, as a new understanding by the believer of himself and of the nature of his humanity. This tension is equally related to the onward course of history and to the reality of the present world in the fullest sense of the word. The faith that in Christ the kingdom appeared and that Jesus is the Son of Man cannot ignore this unredeemed reality in its totality, but must in fact reveal itself as faith in the kingdom in confrontation with this reality. It is seeking, and hoping against hope, for the mercy and justice of God in this world.

5. Finally, as far as the descriptions of the future of the kingdom and the imminence of the parousia of the Son of Man are concerned, it is here that the apocalyptic setting of the gospel comes to the fore in all its strangeness for modern man. Here the relevance of apocalypticism seems very difficult to demonstrate. Certainly the soberness of the New Testament picture of the end-time and the absence of all calculations of the day of the Son of Man are totally different from what is found in some Jewish apocalypses. We are even surprised by the saying (Mark 13:32; Matt. 24:36) that no one knows of that day and that hour, not the angels in heaven nor the Son. But uncertainty over the time does not blot out the repeated talk of imminence nor eclipse the view of the future of the kingdom and the parousia of the Son of Man in the framework of contemporary events. Many have asked how this in many respects ominous description of the end-time and of the imminent end of the world can be in harmony with the liberating overture of the gospel, in which Jesus clearly distances himself from the preaching of judgment of John the Baptist. These are no easy problems, and they become more difficult still when one includes the fourth gospel in the discussion; problems which require a more thorough elaboration than is possible in this brief discussion.

So universal a character does the kingdom of God as starting point of Jesus' preaching bear that even the beatitudes he proclaims in and for this unredeemed world cannot be separated for a moment from the great and cosmic future. The difference between John the Baptist and Jesus is not that the preaching of the former is more and that of the latter less directed to the future. Rather, Jesus distinguishes himself from his predecessor in that he, out of his incomparable consciousness of the nearness of God's grace and love, paved the way to the future in the midst of all the puzzling highs and lows of history, even when the parousia of the Son of Man was delayed. The church, therefore, has to learn to live, to wait, to work by this presence of the grace of God; and that is why the fourth gospel witnesses to the unity of present and future as the hour that comes and is already here. At the same time the Spirit, who is its leader and comforter for the present time, is also the one who, as the Spirit of Christ, urges the church to go forward on the way of the future and to see all that happens on earth in the light of the coming judgment and salvation of the Son of Man.

The question which remains is not whether this expectation of the great future also belongs to the core of the gospel preached by Jesus. The certainty of this future is the overture and finale of the whole New Testament. The real problem also cannot be that Jesus has proclaimed the transcendence of the kingdom in the language of prophecy in apocalyptical visions and representations. It lies rather in this: that the future is seen in such shortened perspective that the time of the longer path of the church, of the preaching of the gospel, is not foreseen. It is this problem of the *Naherwartung*, with which the *theological* exegesis of the New Testament is confronted time and again, and to which it seems to me very difficult to give an adequate answer.

Must we, as some suggest, see here the aftereffect of Jewish apocalypticism, which did not know of the presence of grace in Christ and therefore had no other escape in the tribulations of time than anticipating the future of God? Or must we rather see in this anticipation the mark of a *Christian* faith that was, on the ground of the fulfilment in Christ, so sure of the future that it actually drew the future to itself as a reality which could not be postponed anymore? Perhaps both answers are wrong. Maybe we have to see in that which seems strange and "irrelevant" in this *Naherwartung* the proof of our own incapability to live in the light of the great future, so to live as Christians that we can understand with John that the hour which comes is already near — and even has already come — in the way God is present in his judgments and grace in history. Since Jesus has come, the present and the future can no longer be separated, although the Father holds all things in his own hands and nobody knows the *hour* in which the signs will stop and the trumpet sound; nobody, not even the angels of heaven, not even the Son, but only the Father.

NOTES TO CHAPTER SIX

1. For Bultmann see his essays "New Testament and Mythology," in *Kerygma and Myth*, ed. H. W. Bartsch, Eng. tr. 1961, pp. 1-44; "The Christian Hope and the Problem of Demythologizing," in *Expository Times*, LXV (1954), 228-30, 276-78; and "History and Eschatology in the New Testament," in *New Testament Studies*, I (1954), 5-16.

2. "The Beginnings of Christian Theology," in *New Testament Questions of Today*, Eng. tr. 1969, pp. 82-107, esp. p. 102.

3. Cf. George Eldon Ladd, "Why Not Prophetic-Apocalyptic?", *Journal of Biblical Literature*, LXXVI (1957), 192-200.

4. See Vielhauer, "Gottesreich und Menschensohn in der Verkündigung Jesu," in *Aufsätze zum Neuen Testament*, 1965, pp. 55-91.

5. See, for example, Joachim Jeremias, "Die älteste Schicht der Menschensohn-Logien," *Zeitschrift für die neutestamentliche Wissenschaft*, LVIII (1967), 159-72.

6. *Theological Dictionary of the New Testament*, VIII, Eng. tr. 1972, 400-77.

7. Cf. Bultmann, *Theology of the New Testament*, I, Eng. tr. 1951, 26ff.

8. "Exit the Apocalyptic Son of Man," *New Testament Studies*, IX (1972), 243-67.